The Leadership Framework Series Book 3

MAKE IT WORK!

HOW TO
Successfully Implement Your Business Strategy

PETER MILLS

Make It Work: How to Successfully Implement Your Business Strategy
Peter Mills © 2017

National Library of Australia Cataloguing-in-Publication entry:

Creator:	Mills, Peter, author
Title:	Make It Work: How to Successfully Implement Your Business Strategy / Peter Mills
ISBN:	9781925530698 (paperback)
Series:	Leadership Framework Series; Book 3
Subjects:	Business planning
	Strategic planning.
	Executive ability.
	Management.
	Organizational effectiveness.
	Success in business.

Published by Peter Mills, InHouse Publishing, and GOKO Publishing

Acknowledgments

I WISH TO THANK Barry and Sheila Deane, from PeopleFit Australasia, who developed the original Leadership Framework based on the work of Elliot Jaques and Lord Wilfred Brown. They have kindly given me full access to their substantial and excellent work, without which I could not have written this book.

I also wish to acknowledge Peter Dawe, a retired business studies teacher; George Lagos, a senior business executive; and Therese Harris, a HR professional, whom I have worked with for a number of years; all of whom reviewed early drafts of this book and made valuable suggestions for improvement.

I would also like to thank my wife, Sue, who reviewed the book and was a constant reference point, helping me to clarify my thoughts and ideas.

Using This Book

THIS IS THE THIRD BOOK in a series based on The Leadership Framework, a holistic and integrated framework for managerial leadership.

The first book in the series, *Leading People – The 10 Things Successful Managers Know and Do*, identified what managers, at all levels in an organization, need to know and do to be successful. It focused on the role of the manager and the required accountabilities and authorities for managing people. It detailed how to create effective teams and build the strong manager–team member working relationship required to achieve business goals.

The second book of the series, *Don't Fix Me, Fix the Workplace – A Guide to Building Constructive Working Relationships*, demonstrated how to create the working environment necessary for constructive and productive working relationships. It explained how to create purpose-built organizational structures with specified role relationships and authorized and productive systems of work that, when combined with effective managerial leadership, enable all employees to work together to achieve their business goals.

This third book in *The Leadership Framework Series* is about strategy implementation. The book describes what leaders must do to support successful strategy implementation. After reading this book, the reader will gain a strong understanding of the importance of clearly defining a business strategy and how to align the whole organization, as well as each employee, to support strategy implementation. The reader will not only understand how to implement an organization's strategy, but will also have a clear understanding of the various roles, role relationships and the accountabilities and authorities required for effective strategy implementation.

To assist implementation, each chapter has a clear summary of the key points and some tips for getting started. There is also a companion website available for those who want to access additional information and tools: **www.theleadershipframework.com.au**

This book, like the others, is based on The Leadership Framework. Therefore you will find the concepts in all the books in the series are aligned and use consistent terms, definitions, principles, concepts, methods and processes.

Each book gives focus to one area of managerial leadership. Used together, they are a powerful tool for leaders at all levels.

Contents

Chapter 1

About Strategy

*Strategy describes what an organization
is attempting to accomplish over a
period of years, as represented by the
organization's collective objectives.*

EACH YEAR MOST ORGANIZATIONS turn their attention to strategic planning, where the leadership team comes together to plan the organization's future. The leadership team often take a one- or two-day retreat and then, over the next few months, formulate the organization's three- to five-year strategic plan. It will be used to guide the organization's future and to solve its problems. It's new and they are excited.

And then? Nothing but talk or blame as to why it wasn't implemented. The following year the process starts again and there is a new "strategy".

Why did it fail? Because the leadership team didn't build execution into their strategic planning process. They failed to set the organization up for success.

Good strategic planning doesn't end with strategy creation, it ends with implementation. Unless done well, even the best strategy will fail, and the time and effort taken to create it will be wasted. More critically, the organization will not do what it needed to do to be successful.

The focus of this book is on strategy implementation, not strategy development. It is important, however, to understand what strategy is and is not. Put simply:

Strategy describes what an organization is attempting to accomplish over a period of years, as represented by the organization's collective objectives.

A strategy specifies what you do and don't do. It results in initiatives designed to achieve defined objectives. Furthermore, strategy is a long-term commitment. Strategic initiatives take time to implement. Initiatives such as developing new workforce competencies, redefining a brand, creating new product lines, building new customer relationships and reengineering key business processes cannot be implemented quickly.

Furthermore, strategy implementation often requires trade-offs, as gains in one area can often only be achieved at the expense of another area.

Strategic vs Operational Effectiveness

Strategic effectiveness and operational effectiveness are both essential for superior performance, but they are different. Strategy exists to drive change, and its resulting initiatives are discretionary to day-to-day work. Strategy requires an organization to make trade-offs; to choose what to do and what not to do.

Operational initiatives are not discretionary, they are part of day-to-day work. Operational excellence means performing similar activities better than competitors, i.e. performing the myriad of activities that go into creating, producing, selling and delivering the organization's products and services.

Why Strategy Implementation Fails

While a good strategy is a great start, organizations must be able to deliver on their intent. Unfortunately, many organizations are not very good at this. Strategy involves change, and change is difficult. Human tendency is to resist it. So, no matter how inspiring a new strategic vision is or how fantastic the products or innovative the technology, it will come up against hurdles. Only solid execution will put an organization on the competitive map.

There are many reasons why strategy implementation plan fails. The most common are:

- **An overwhelming strategic plan:** Managers don't know where to begin. The goals and initiatives generated in the strategic planning process are too numerous because the leadership team failed to make tough choices to eliminate non-critical actions.
- **Unrealistic goals:** While strategic objectives may stretch the organization, they still must be realistic. If people feel the goals are unachievable they may not try.
- **Lack of leadership:** This issue is at multiple levels. It is not only about ensuring that each manager at each level is clear about the accountabilities and authorities they have for strategy implementation, it is about all managers understanding their role as a people manager.
- **Focus on structural changes:** Many organizations overly rely on structural change to execute strategy. While changing structure has its place, it is only part of the requirement for successful strategy implementation.
- **Unclear accountability:** If people are not clear of their role and their accountabilities for strategy delivery, or are not held accountable for their work, it'll be business as usual for all but a few frustrated individuals. Clear accountability helps drive change.

- **Lack of empowerment:** Accountability needs matching authority to deliver outcomes. It also needs the tools and resources necessary to achieve strategic initiatives.
- **Lack of communication:** Communication helps with organizational alignment. If a plan doesn't get communicated to employees, they won't understand their role or how they contribute to achieving the organization's strategy.
- **Getting caught up in the day-to-day:** Managers are often consumed by daily operational problems and lose sight of long-term goals. Unless there is an organizational focus on strategy implementation, managers will focus on their day-to-day work.
- **Lack of clarity on actions required:** The actions required to execute the strategy are not specified or clearly defined.
- **Inadequate monitoring:** Managers are unable to assess if the strategy is being achieved. Without clear information on how and why performance is falling short, it is virtually impossible to take appropriate action.
- **No progress reporting:** There's no method to track progress, or the plan only measures what's easy, not what's important, so no one feels any forward momentum.
- **Lack of alignment:** The organization has not been aligned for strategy implementation. Organizational silos and culture blocks execution and/or organizational processes don't support strategic requirements.

These issues can be overcome by using a planned, step-by-step approach to strategy implementation. This book uses the principles and practices of The Leadership Framework, a holistic and integrated system of managerial leadership, as the basis for strategy implementation (see Appendix 1).

Key Concepts

- Strategy describes what an organization is attempting to accomplish over a period of years, as represented by the organization's collective objectives.
- A good strategy is a great start. However, organizations must be able to deliver on their intent, and only solid execution will put an organization on the competitive map.
- Strategy involves change, and change is difficult. Human tendency is to resist it.
- While there are many barriers to successful strategy implementation, these barriers can be overcome by using a planned, step-by-step approach to strategy implementation.

Tips for Getting Started

1. Review 'Why Strategy Implementation Fails' in this chapter. Identify three issues that you feel impact strategy implementation in your organization or business. Write these down and assess possible solutions at the end of each of the following chapters.

Additional information available at: www.theleadershipframework.com.au

1. Implement business strategy.
2. Understand your role.
3. What is a working organization?

Chapter 2

The Strategy Implementation Process – An Overview

Strategic planning defines what an organization believes it must do to be successful and why. Strategy implementation is about converting strategic objectives into clear initiatives and aligning the organization to deliver the strategy, i.e. how, who, when and where.

DELIVERING STRATEGY HAS TWO PARTS: strategic planning and strategy implementation. The strategic planning process addresses the *why* and *what* an organization needs to change to be successful. The outcome of this process is a set of strategic objectives for implementation.

Strategy implementation is about converting these strategic objectives into initiatives to deliver the strategic plan, i.e. *how, who, when* and *where*. Competitive advantage is only gained when both planning and implementation are performed well.

The process to plan a strategy and implement that strategy is summarized in the diagram below.

Developing & implementing strategy

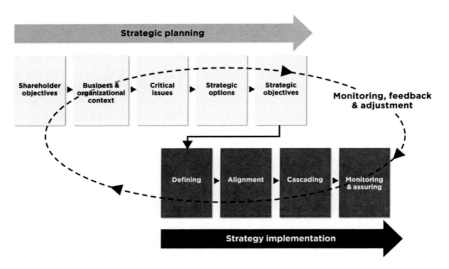

Strategy Implementation

Strategy implementation begins after the strategic planning process has been completed, i.e. when all strategic options have been assessed and a set of strategic objectives is produced.

Strategy implementation has four steps:

1. **Defining the strategy:** Clarifying strategic objectives and their related initiatives so they can be implemented (see Chapter 3: The Strategy Implementation Process – Defining the Strategy).

2. **Aligning the organization:** Getting the organization ready for strategy deployment by aligning the working organization to support strategy implementation, connecting planning and budgeting and allocating

accountability and authority at a high level (see 'Chapter 4: The Strategy Implementation Process – Aligning the Organization for Strategy Deployment').

3. **Cascading work:** Engaging employees and assigning tasks with appropriate measures throughout the organization (see Chapter 5: The Strategy Implementation Process – Cascading and Deploying Strategy).

4. **Monitoring and assuring strategy implementation:** Reviewing the progress of strategy implementation and the effectiveness of the strategy itself (see Chapter 6: The Strategy Implementation Process – Monitoring and Assuring the Strategy).

Each step is performed in the context of a *working organization*, so before directly outlining each step of strategy implementation, it is important to understand the components of a working organization.

The Working Organization

Good strategy implementation is the result of the thousands of decisions made every day by employees, acting in accordance with the information they have. This information comes through the working organization. Working organizations exist to coordinate the work of many people toward a common business purpose, i.e. to produce the organization's products and/or services.

In efforts to implement a new strategy, many organizations go straight to structural changes, as these changes are immediately visible and are seen as concrete. It shows that action is occurring. But organizations are more complex than this. The implementation of business strategy often requires adjustments to all aspects of the working organization, as it is the whole organization that impacts people, culture and strategy delivery. So, what are the critical parts of the working organization?

Working organizations have physical assets; however, strategy is delivered by people working together. This work is coordinated through the organization's structure (functions, roles and role relationships) and its systems of work (policies, processes and information and communication technologies) with the application of effective managerial leadership practices. Each component provides the context for people's work, and together they create the working environment that impacts upon the effectiveness of all employees, including managers (see diagram below).

The working organization

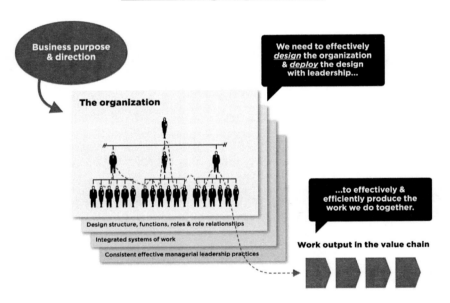

In brief, the working organization is made up of:

i.   Business purpose and direction.

The direction of a working organization is defined by the organization's business purpose, part of which is its strategy. An organization's purpose and direction provides the focus and context for all work, with strategy specifying what the organization will and will not do.

Without this focus, the context of people's work will be confused and unproductive work will occur. There will be a lack of prioritization of projects and a waste of time, effort and resources. There will be confusion on what is important to the organization, and therefore people's day-to-day work. This resultant confusion will impact on strategy implementation.

ii.   Structure, functions, roles and role relationship.

To deliver its purpose and strategy, roles are created and organized into functions. An organization's structure provides the shared understanding of accountability and authority that exists between people whose work is aligned and integrated with other roles to deliver the organization's products and services in line with the strategy. Each role has a specific purpose, with specific accountabilities and authorities that enable people to work together effectively and collaboratively. These roles are commonly represented on paper as a two-dimensional organization chart.

- The horizontal dimension illustrates how work is organized into core functions, such as sales, service and manufacturing, and how this work is supported by specialist functions such as finance and human resources.
- The vertical layers reflect the complexity of work at different levels, and that work in organizations occurs over differing time periods; with each layer adding value in a different way.

When well designed, the right type of work will be performed at the right level by the right roles, and each role will have clear accountabilities with matching authority for the work. If poorly designed, there will be gaps or duplication of effort, and there will be misaligned accountabilities and authorities for work. This has the potential to cause unnecessary conflict and loss of focus on what is important to the organization.

 iii. Systems of work.

Systems of work provide "standardizing" methods for work to be done to deliver an organization's products and services. They consist of the organization's policies, procedures, processes and information and communication technologies. They enable roles to work together, within teams, across teams and across the organization. They enable roles (people) to work together to deliver the organization's purpose and direction (strategy).

If well designed, systems of work will assist with strategy implementation and enable effective allocation of resources and tools to deliver and monitor strategy implementation. When poorly designed and/or poorly implemented, systems of work will not support or will adversely impact strategy implementation.

 iv. Effective managerial leadership.

In a working organization, managers at every level must be able to achieve the business goal set for them in line with the organization's strategy. Managers:

- Build teams that are capable and committed to achieving business outcomes.
- Set the purpose and direction for their team and enable team members to move together in that direction with competence, commitment and enthusiasm.
- Provide the environment that allows their team to be effective and satisfied in the work while developing their full potential.
- Design and deploy the organization's structure, roles, role relationships and systems of work.

To achieve these outcomes, managers must apply effective management practices.

To ensure a successful strategy implementation, each part of the working organization must be aligned and integrated to operate effectively. Without clear direction; an effective structure (with clearly defined roles and role relationships); and integrated systems of work, all activated by effective managerial leadership practices, the organization's strategy and purpose may not be delivered. The causes of failure will not be clear. Focus will be on individuals and not the working organization.

Strategy and Culture

A book on strategy implementation would not be complete without touching on organizational culture. Culture is the shared assumptions and beliefs a group of people has about certain behaviors based on what that group values or does not value. The more beliefs people share, the stronger the culture. Culture gives people a framework within which they can begin to organize their world and their behavior. Put simply, culture is the accepted standards of behavior, i.e. "the way we do things around here".

While all employees come to work with a complete set of values, preferences, and inhibitors (VP&I), an innate level of work ability (LoWA) and their knowledge, skills, and experience (KSE), their behavior, and therefore an organization's culture, is impacted by the working organization, i.e. the organization's:

- Managerial leadership practices and behavior of managers in the organization;
- The organization's systems, which include its structure; and
- The symbols created in relation to the above, such as recognition, uniforms, car parks and rewards.

The following diagram outlines these impacts on employee behavior.

Impacts on employee behavior

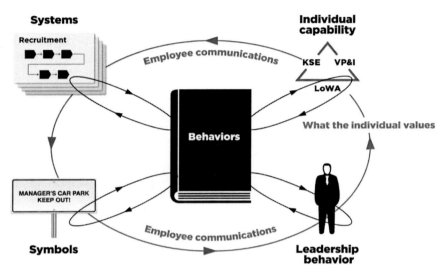

Note: In the above diagram, organizational design is part of *Systems*.

While not wanting to understate the role of managers in creating culture, the importance of systems, including organizational structure, in creating culture should not be underestimated. An organization's leadership team defines and sustains its culture through what it values and embeds through the design and deployment of its structure and systems of work, i.e. its rules, regulations, policies, procedures, and symbols. These are the things that create custom, practices, traditions, beliefs and assumptions and create standards and expectations on how work is done. They are a significant influence on how people experience work.

Leadership that is dependent on role modeling alone will not last, as behavior will revert unless it is reinforced by a system of work. This is because systems of work and structure:

- Reinforce what is valued in the organization.
- Embed required behavior in the processes and, as processes are repeated, like habits, employees get used to them and act according to their requirements— "It's the way we do things around here."
- Operate all the time, all day, every day. Unlike the manager, they are ever-present.

It is the working organization that drives culture, so changes to any aspect of the working organization will impact an organization's culture and the effectiveness of its strategy implementation.

Key Concepts

- The starting point for strategy implementation is after strategy planning has been completed.
- A strategic plan addresses *what* an organization needs to do and *why*. Strategy implementation addresses *how, who, when* and *where*.
- Strategy implementation has four steps:
  - ➢ Defining the strategy—clarifying strategic objectives and the related initiatives.
  - ➢ Aligning the organization—getting ready for deployment.
  - ➢ Cascading work to relevant employees.
  - ➢ Monitoring and assuring strategy implementation.
- Working organizations exist to coordinate the work of many people toward a common business purpose. Managers need to understand the impacts of the whole working organization to be able to implement business strategy.

- Leadership dependent on role modeling alone will not last, as behavior will revert unless it is reinforced by structure and a system of work.
- Changes to the working organization will impact organizational culture and strategy implementation.

Tips for Getting Started

1. Consider the nature of a working organization. How does it impact your team?
2. The work environment critically influences an individual's ability to do their best work. Identify aspects of the work environment that impact your team's ability to deliver the organization's strategy.
3. If you are interested in organizational impacts on employees working together, read *Don't Fix Me, Fix the Workplace – A Guide to Building Constructive Working Relationships* by Peter Mills.

Additional information available at: www.theleadershipframework.com.au

1. Implement business strategy.
2. Design the organization.
3. Design and maintain productive systems of work.
4. Role of the manager.
5. Understand the role of others.

Chapter 3

The Strategy Implementation Process – Defining the Strategy

> *Defining the strategy is about clearly articulating what must be done for an organization's future success. It involves clarifying strategic objectives, prioritizing related initiatives and ensuring resources are available so the initiatives can be implemented.*

THE FIRST STEP in strategy implementation is to define the strategy. While it could be argued that creating strategic objectives (the last step in the strategic planning process) and defining them are part of the same process, defining the strategy is about clarifying *how* each strategic objective will be implemented. It allows everyone to understand what the organization sees as important and where the organization is committing its resources. It provides context for the work of all employees, i.e. Where are we heading? What's my part? How is my performance measured?

Defining the strategy

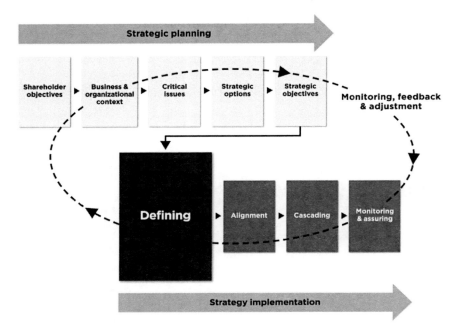

To accurately define a strategy requires the leadership team to:

- Cleary describe each objective, i.e. what the organization will and won't do.
- Create and define measures for each objective.
- Set targets for each objective.
- Turn strategic objectives into prioritized and funded initiatives.

Describing Each Objective

Although the strategy is described in the strategic planning process, all too often it is expressed as high-level statements that resonate with boards and executive levels but fall flat with the people accountable for doing the work. Strategic objectives must describe the strategy in a way that people in the organization can understand, support and implement. Therefore, keep it simple and avoid drawn out descriptions of grand goals or objectives so that the organization's future direction is clear to all.

Clearly describing the strategy also assists with:

- The creation of suitable measures and targets for each strategic objective.
- The development of appropriate initiatives to deliver strategic objectives.
- The allocation of accountability and authority to the right roles.
- Effective communication to all employees.

Clearly describing strategic objectives may also reveal issues of organizational alignment, such as the need to adjust the organization's structure or relevant systems of work.

Creating and Defining Measures for Each Strategic Objective

Each strategic objective requires a measure. Measures provide clarity to vague concepts and facilitate the effective monitoring and assuring of progress. They are indicators of 'where we are' at some point in time.

There are four types of measures: cost, quality, quantity and timeliness. For a measure to be fit for purpose there must be a distinct relationship between the objective and its measure(s). While it may not always be possible to have a direct one-to-one relationship, measures can still be useful indicators of performance. Obviously the stronger the relationship between the objective and its measure, the better.

To facilitate effective monitoring and assurance of strategy implementation, it is important for selected measures to monitor both outcomes and drivers of performance. These are often called lag and lead measures. Outcome measures focus on results at the end of a timeframe while driver measures focus on items that drive the achievement of an objective. Balancing outcome and driver measures ensures early warning of things going off track.

Examples of each type of measure are shown in the table below.

Outcome Measures vs Driver Measures

	Outcome measure (lag)	Driver measure (lead)
Purpose	To focus on the performance results at the end of a time period or activity. Was the objective achieved?	To measure intermediate processes, activity or behavior that leads to achieving an objective.
Example	• Year-end sales. • Market share.	• Hours spent with customers. • Revenue mix.
Strengths	• Usually objective and easily captured.	• More predictive in nature. • Allows organizations to adjust actions and behaviors toward improved performance.
Issues	• Outcome measures reflect success of past, not current activities and decisions.	• Based on hypotheses of cause and effect. • Often difficult to collect supporting data.

Setting Targets

To clearly define a strategic objective, each objective must not only have a measure, it must be assigned a target. A target defines the desired level of improvement required to achieve the objective. Targets focus the organization and its employees on the actions and the required behaviors to achieve each strategic objective.

Measures and targets enable organizations to track progress toward achieving strategic objectives. They compare current levels of performance with required levels of performance and, as such, they enable monitoring, adjustment and feedback. Targets inform managers if an objective or initiative has been achieved. Without targets, measures have a limited value.

The main four methods of setting targets are:

- Derived from the objective.
- Comparison to a benchmark.
- Incremental improvement from the previous period.
- Establish a baseline and define targets in the future.

An example of each method is shown in the table below.

Methods of Target Setting

Target setting method	Objective	Measure	Target Current year	Target Next year
Derived from objective	Increase annual revenue to $41,000	Annual revenue	$40,000	$41,000
Comparison to a benchmark	Achieve benchmark performance for customer satisfaction (90%)	Industry benchmark	80%	90%
Incremental improvement from previous period	Reduce defects rate by 1%	Percent of defects	5%	4%
Establish baseline and define targets over time	Improve employee engagement score by 5%	Complete staff survey (to establish a baseline)	Establish current (baseline) level	Baseline plus 5%

Once measures and targets have been selected, it is good practice to create a *measure definition table*. A measures definition table contains all relevant information for an objective's measures and targets. A template for a measure definition table is shown in the table below.

Measure Definition Table		
Name of measure:		
Purpose of measure and link to strategy: (The strategic objective or initiative the measure aligns to and why it is an appropriate measure)		
Definition:		
Units:	**Method of calculation:**	
Frequency of updates:	**Frequency of reporting:**	**Method of reporting:**
Milestones: (if appropriate)		**Target:**
Clients/customers:		**Owner/ custodian:**
Accountability for updates: **Accountability for reporting:**		

Creating a measure definition table:

- Ensures that rigor has been put into selecting the right measure for each strategic objective.
- Provides clarity on each strategic objective's measure and how they are calculated.
- Enables all stakeholders to understand how the measure links to the organization's strategy.
- Informs stakeholders of who is accountable for reporting on the measure and how often.
- Supports effective communication of the strategy.

For organizational reference, all corporate measures should be collated into one document: a *measures dictionary*. This document enables managers to refer to specific measures and understand what the organization is trying to achieve and how they, as managers, support an objectives delivery.

Using measures and targets to communicate business performance is also a powerful way to engage people in the business. For employees, they help answer the question "Where we are going?"

Turning Strategic Objectives Into Prioritized and Funded Initiatives

Once the organization's strategic objectives, measures and targets are set, the CEO and leadership team must decide on the initiatives required to achieve each strategic objective. An initiative is an intervention to move the organization from its current state to a desired future state. The aim is to close a performance gap. It is why initiatives exist.

Example of an Initiative

Strategic objective		Initiative
What?	**Why?**	**How?**
Improve customer satisfaction.	Research shows that when customers continually receive an incorrect invoice they go to other suppliers. The current billing system has a high error rate resulting in a high level of customer complaints.	Replace the current customer billing system.

The creation of an initiative also requires the allocation of resources. Resources include people, time and money, and these resources are limited. Resources are allocated as part of the whole of organization budgeting process. Often funds are not be available to implement all the required initiatives so choices need to be made. It is therefore necessary to assess all current and proposed initiatives against the organization's strategic objectives to ensure that:

- Each strategic objective has an appropriate initiative to move the organization to the required level of performance.
- All initiatives are approved.
- Each initiative is allocated enabling resources and that these resources are budgeted.
- All current initiatives are focused on achieving current strategic objectives (so that resources are not wasted).

To make this assessment, an initiative alignment matrix is created. The matrix highlights:

- Initiatives that are using resources but have little benefit for achievement of the strategy.

- Objectives that do not have suitable initiatives.
- The availability of resources to deliver each initiative.

From the initiative alignment matrix, the CEO and leadership team can assess and optimize the allocation of resources to deliver the strategy. An example of an initiative alignment matrix is shown below.

Example Initiative Alignment Matrix

Strategic objectives			Current initiatives									
	Measure	Target	Initiative A	Initiative B	Initiative C	Initiative D	Initiative E	Initiative F	Initiative G	Initiative H	Initiative I	Initiative J
Objective 1	y	y+	X									
Objective 2	y	y+										
Objective 3	y	y+		X		X		X				
Objective 4	y	y+					X					
Objective 5	y	y+										
Objective 6	y	y+							X			
Objective 7	y	y+									X	
Objective 8	y	y+										
Objective 9	y	y+								X		
Objective 10	y	y+										X
Resourcing available			Y	Y	Y	Y	Y	N	Y	Y	Y	Y

In the example, Strategic Objectives 2, 5 and 8 have no initiatives (an under allocation of resources) while Strategic Objective 3 has three initiatives (possibly an over allocation of resources). Also, Initiative C does not map to any Strategic Objective. It must therefore be assessed as to its need and priority.

For Initiative F, resourcing is not readily available. In this instance the CEO and leadership team will have to decide to either provide resources or drop the initiative. If they decide to drop the initiative, they must consider the impact it will have on achieving the objective (Strategic Objective 3).

The effective combination of strategic objectives, measures, targets and resourced initiatives articulates to everyone in the organization where the organization currently is, where it plans to be and what it needs to do to get there. It sets the context for each person's work. It helps employees connect to the strategy. Defining the strategy also lays the foundation for organizational alignment, which is the next step in the strategy implementation process.

Key Concepts

- Defining the strategy is the first of the four steps in strategy implementation. It uses the outputs of the strategic planning process as the inputs for strategy implementation.
- Defining the strategy is about clarifying strategic objectives and their related initiatives so they can be implemented. This is achieved by:
  - Cleary describing each strategic objective, i.e. what the organization will and won't do.
  - Creating and defining measures for each strategic objective.
  - Setting targets for each strategic objective.
  - Turning strategic objectives into prioritized and funded initiatives.
- Each objective needs to be described in a way so that people in the organization can understand it, support it and implement it.

- Measures are indicators of 'where we are' at some point in time. They provide clarity to vague concepts and facilitate the effective monitoring and assuring of progress.
- A target defines the desired level of improvement required to achieve an objective. Targets focus the organization and individuals on the actions and required behaviors needed to achieve strategic objectives.
- It is good practice to create a measure definition table for each measure and associated target. For organizational reference, all corporate measures should be collated into one document: a measures dictionary. This document enables managers to refer to specific measures, understand what the organization is trying to achieve and how they, as managers, support the objectives delivery.
- The CEO and leadership team must decide on the initiatives required to achieve each objective. An initiative is an intervention to move the organization from the current state to the future desired level of performance.
- Defining the strategy lays the foundation for organizational alignment—the next step in the strategy implementation process.

Tips for Getting Started

1. Review one of your organization's strategic objectives. Is the required outcome clear? If not, why not?
2. Does the selected strategic objective have clear measures and appropriate targets?
3. For the selected strategic objective, identify the initiatives to deliver it. Assess the likely impact of these initiatives on the achievement of the strategic objective.

Additional information available at www.theleadershipframework.com.au

1. What is work?
2. How managers align work.
3. How to effectively assign a task.
4. How to effectively assess work.

Chapter 4

The Strategy Implementation Process – Aligning the Organization for Strategy Deployment

*Aligning the working organization to
implement strategic objectives is critical.
There must be clear accountability and
authority for action and an environment
that enables success.*

ONCE THE PROCESS of defining the strategy has been completed, the process of organizational alignment can commence. The aim of organizational alignment is to:

- Allocate accountability and authority at a high level.
- Connect planning and budgeting.
- Align the working organization to support strategy implementation.

Aligning the strategy

Allocating Accountability and Authority for Initiatives

A critical requirement for the organization of work is that every person, in every role, at every level, is clear on what work they must do to play their part. The blurring of accountability and authority is fatal for strategy implementation. It can result in:

- Important decisions not being made or becoming stalled or negotiated between functions or individuals.
- Overlapping work boundaries, resulting in confusion, uncertainty and an inappropriate use of authority.
- A misallocation of resources to complete an initiative.

All of this impedes information flow, hinders productive work and promotes workarounds. People will continue to work on the things they do best, i.e. their day-to-day operational work, and forget about strategic outcomes.

The allocation of accountability and authority starts with the leadership team. Each strategic initiative must be assigned an owner at the executive level, i.e. a person who is accountable for the initiative and who has the authority to implement it. It is the accountability of the CEO to assign this ownership to relevant leaders.

Where an initiative requires action from multiple divisions, the CEO must break the initiative up and assign accountability for each component. The CEO then allocates these components as part of the business planning process; once again clarifying accountability and authority to deliver the task. Each task will require its own measure and target for achievement.

To ensure all initiatives are allocated, an organizational alignment table, such as the one on the following page, is created.

Organization

			Core services			Support services			External
Objective	Measure	Initiatives	Div A	Div B	Div C	Div E	Div F	Div G	External
Objective 1	xx	Initiative 1	X						
		Initiative 2	X						
Objective 2	xx	Initiative 3		X					
		Initiative 4		X					
Objective 3	xx	Initiative 5			X				
Objective 4	xx	Initiative 6				X			
		Initiative 7					X		
Objective 5	xx	Initiative 8 - Part A						X	
		Initiative 8 - Part B					X		
		Initiative 9							X

This process allows each member of the leadership team to understand who is accountable to deliver the organization's strategy.

Having established who is accountable, the person in the role must then be provided with the authorities they need to deliver their accountabilities. Authorities are those aspects of a role that enable the person in the role to act legitimately to carry out their accountabilities. They include the authority to expend certain defined resources (including their own time), work with other people, get access to information and to instruct others in the organization.

Connecting Planning to Budgeting

The process of allocating accountability and authority includes the process of allocating resources and the necessary budget for allocated initiatives. These resources would have been approved at an organizational level during the first step of strategy implementation—"Define the strategy".

It is at this point the organization needs to make the decision as to whether the approved resources for each initiative are to be integrated into the accountable manager's budget or if a separate strategy execution budget is to be maintained. This decision comes down to how the organization wants to monitor strategy implementation.

Aligning the Working Organization to Support Strategy Implementation

To support strategy implementation, the whole working organization must be reviewed and, if necessary, adjusted. Effective strategy implementation requires work to be organized and delegated to the right people, at the right level and in the right roles. These roles must be designed to work together, as roles tell people what they are supposed to do and what they are entitled to expect from others (see Chapter 7: Strategy Implementation and Structure).

It also requires systems of work, i.e. the organization's policies, procedures, forms, information and communication technologies, be aligned, as systems of work coordinate and direct the work of the organization's people to deliver its products and services (see Chapter 8: Strategy and Implementation Systems of Work).

Finally, it requires the alignment of managerial practices, as managers activate strategy, structure and systems of work (see Chapter 9: Strategy Implementation and Effective Managerial Leadership).

Once accountability, authority and resourcing at a high level has been allocated and the organization has decided the changes required to the structure, systems of work and managerial leadership to implement the strategy, the cascading of objectives can commence.

Key Concepts

- A critical requirement for strategy implementation is that every person, in every role, at every level, is clear on what work they must do to play their part. The blurring of accountability and authority is fatal for strategy implementation. The allocation of accountability and authority starts with the leadership team.
- Each strategic initiative needs an owner at the executive level; a person who is accountable for the initiative and who has the authority to implement it. It is the CEO who is accountable to assign clear tasks to relevant leaders to ensure strategy implementation.
- Where an initiative requires action from multiple divisions, the CEO must break the initiative into components and

create individual task assignments for each VP/general manager.

- Having established who is accountable, the person in the role must then be provided with the authorities they need to deliver their accountabilities. The process of allocating accountability and authority includes the process of allocating resources, including the necessary budget for allocated initiatives.
- All aspects of the working organization support strategy delivery. Therefore, the organization's structure, systems of work and managerial leadership must be reviewed and, if necessary, adjusted.

Tips for Getting Started

1. Review your organization's strategic initiatives. Is it clear who is accountable for each strategic initiative?
   a. If yes, does this role have the authority and resources to implement the initiative?
   b. If no, determine what impacts this may have on strategy implementation.

Additional information available at www.theleadershipframework.com.au

1. Design the organization.
2. Design and maintain productive systems of work.
3. Create effective roles and put good people in them.
4. Effectively assign and assess work.

Chapter 5

The Strategy Implementation Process – Cascading and Deploying the Strategy

Cascading the strategy involves moving work down the organization. It is about engaging employees in strategy delivery, with managers converting complex work into less complex tasks and allocating them to team members with the accountability, authority and resources needed to complete the tasks.

ONCE THE ALLOCATION of accountability, authority and resources at a high level has been completed, cascading the strategy can begin. Cascading the strategy is a continual process of engaging employees in the strategy by breaking up the complex work into less complex tasks. These tasks are then allocated to each employee, together with the appropriate accountability, authority and necessary resources to complete each task.

Cascading the strategy

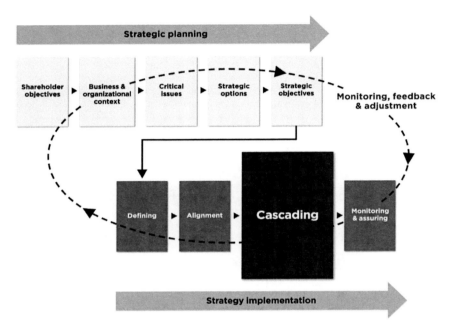

By breaking up the work and allocating tasks down the organization, strategy becomes linked to day-to-day work.

Successful strategy implementation requires every employee to know what they are expected to deliver and how. Specifically, they must know:

1. Where are we going?
   (What is our direction? What are our priorities? What do we need to do to be successful?)
2. What's my role?
   (What is my part in this?)
3. How will my performance be measured or judged?
   (What does success look like? How effective have I been in delivering on my commitments?)

Cascading moves strategy implementation from an organizational level to an individual level, as shown in the table below.

	Objective	Initiative	Measure	Target
For organization	What does the strategy achieve? What is critical to success?	What will be done to close the gap?	How will progress be measured and tracked?	What is the level of performance or rate of improvement needed?
For individual	Where are we going?	What is my role?	How is performance measured?	

The Cascading Process

To effectively cascade the strategy, organizations must:

i.   Communicate the strategy.

Formal communication programs help employees understand the strategy. It helps them understand how their day-to-day choices affect the organization's required outcomes, as rational decisions are necessarily bounded by the information available.

A broad-based communication program shares the strategic objectives with all employees and supports the cascading process by setting the context and purpose of any change. It is not about allocating work, it is about providing the big picture.

Onetime events, such as the distribution of brochures or holding of meetings, to kick off a program are fine but they are not sufficient for strategy communication. What is required is the use of multiple mediums, such as internal blogs, message boards, podcasts and department meetings. The aim is to communicate what the strategy is and how it will impact everyone's work.

Remember, in the communication of any change:

- Communicate early, before rumors start.
- Be open—don't keep secrets.
- Avoid grand announcements—the more formal, the more likely it will fail.
- Resist gathering employees into large groups.
- Provide a broad overview but refine the message to the audience.

Also, communicate those things that are important to the employees; the things they are concerned and passionate about. Employees outside the leadership team are not overly concerned with:

- How profits are used.
- Financial results.
- Advertising and promotional plans.
- Operations outside their department or division, except as part of the context.

Provide each team with the big picture as it relates to their work. Doing this sets the context for work by providing team members with a broad understanding of what is going on, so they can make informed decisions on their work.

ii. Set the context and direction for work—three levels working together.

For successful strategy implementation, the context and direction of work must be integrated across teams. It is the accountability of each employee's manager-once-removed (MOR) to integrate work across their team of teams. The role of the MOR is to ensure their direct reporting managers collaborate to achieve the business unit's plans.

One of the ways they do this is by MORs holding meetings with their immediate subordinate managers together with their manager's team members. The aim of these meetings is to provide an understanding of where each team fits into the work of the overall business unit. The meetings also ensure the MOR's team of teams understand that their managers are being supported in their work.

Three levels working together
Stratum V organization

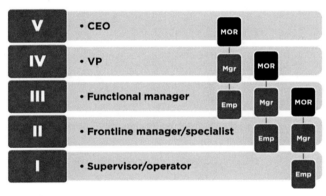

Legend

MOR - Manager-once-removed
Mgr - Manager
Emp - Employee

When these three levels are together, the MOR discusses corporate strategies and how they impact the work of the function. These meetings provide the group with a sense of where the business is going and are an opportunity to discuss problem areas. They facilitate the flow of information across departmental boundaries and up and down the organization's structure.

iii. Cascade with *value-adding engagement*.

All employees need to be engaged in strategy implementation. Cascading with value-adding engagement allows for input by team members, which improves idea generation and engages the team and, as such, improves the chances for successful strategy implementation. It also improves task assignment and the allocation of the right work to the right level and the right role.

Value-adding engagement requires every manager, at every level, to review the initiatives they have been allocated and to discuss implementation with their team. They discuss *what* must be achieved and *why* it must be achieved. Input is then received from team members on *how* these requirements can be achieved. The diagram below outlines the process of value-adding engagement.

The planning process
Cascading the plan

Value-adding engagement; clarifying 'why', 'what' & 'how'

When the value-adding engagement process is completed, the manager decides what will be done and how it will be done. The manager then begins to align the work of their team by breaking the strategic goals/initiatives into component tasks for delivery.

iv. Align the work.

Aligning work across team members is where managers break down complex objectives or tasks into component tasks so they are ready to be allocated. The aim is to transform the manager's strategic objectives and initiatives to understandable and contextualized work for each individual, ensuring that everyone knows where they fit in the plan.

In making these decisions, managers must decide whether the whole task is to be assigned to an individual or whether a subset of the task is assigned for completion. This will depend on the design of the role, the capability of the assignee and the time available. In all cases, the manager must be clear about the scope and boundaries of the work assigned.

In the following example the general manager of Human Resources has a goal to improve safety performance. After discussions on the *what*, *why* and *how* with team members, the delivery of this goal is broken down by the general manager and relevant component tasks are allocated to each team member.

Divisional goal/initiative: Improve safety performance			
Goal/Initiative	Safety manager	Organizational development manager	Planning and reporting manager
Provide leadership in safety.	Launch safety strategy.		Integrate safety leadership into Strategic Workforce Plan.
Develop clear accountabilities and authorities for safety.	Define accountabilities for safety across the organization.	Develop training program on safety accountabilities.	
Improve hazard identification and risk control.	Implement improved hazard identification and risk control processes.		
Develop effective measurement systems.	Develop positive measures for safety.		Develop new safety reports based on positive measures.

When the alignment process is completed individual tasks can be assigned.

v.   Effectively assign tasks.

Tasks can be assigned independently or as part of the organization's performance planning process. Either way it is essential to ensure each team member has a clear understanding of the work to be performed. People perform their best work when they are:

- Clear about the goal.
- Clear about what is expected and the boundaries within which they work.
- Given some freedom to determine how they are going to achieve their goals.
- Able to contribute to the development of the task assignment.

This means they need a clear understanding of the: context, purpose, quality and quantity required for each task. They must also have a clear understanding of the resources available for task completion and the time the task is due.

The application of this CPQQRT method for assigning a task requires managers to provide the following for each task:

- *Context (Why?)*
  This explains why this work needs to be done, how it fits with the team's business direction and other goals, tasks or issues that need to be considered to complete the task. The aim is to provide a good background of the problem to be addressed, including any work completed to date.
- *Purpose (What?)*
  This defines what is to be delivered. This is usually one sentence, e.g. "To design a graduate recruitment process."
- *Quantity (How much?)*
  There is always a quantity involved in an output, therefore it must be specified, e.g. "Produce two marketing brochures per market per region."
- *Quality (How well?)*
  Specifying the quality required is essential, otherwise there is significant room for varying interpretation.

Quality includes the criteria for success. A practical way to express task quality is for the manager to describe (subjectively, as well as objectively through measures) what they believe "a good job" would look like when it is completed.

- **R**esources *(Resources to deliver)*
  Managers will need to assign resources in terms of the financial, material, technical (systems and processes) or people that can be used to complete the task.
- **T**ime *(By when?)*
  There will always be a time when a task must be completed. It is a requirement that this time be explicitly stated in the task assignment. There are two primary reasons for this:
  - ➢ The person will most likely have other tasks to complete during the new tasks timeframe. Providing a clear deadline for a task allows the person to plan their work in the most effective manner to meet the commitment or to discuss any concerns around the timeframe.
  - ➢ When the time allowed for the task is stated explicitly, the manager and team member have a common understanding when the output is expected. If either the manager or team member learns new information that affects the team member's ability to complete the task within the specified timeframe, they can discuss it and determine if changes need to be made to the task assignment.

Correctly assigning tasks is not a one-way process. The process is iterative: manager and team member engage in a discussion about the work to be done until the task's requirements are clear. Asking for input on a task and taking suggestions not only improves the understanding but also the outcome of the task. Having a CPQQRT helps establish trust in assigning work and enables fairness when assessing that work. It is one of the ways a manager builds trust and engagement in the work.

In the task assignment process, employees are accountable to clarify and check their understanding on the tasks, offer suggestions to improve the outcomes,and renegotiate elements of the task that they think cannot be achieved. In carrying out the work they are accountable to give feedback on progress, raise any issues that may impact on the completion of the task and to work within the limits.

Engaging team members in the task allocation process enables them to use their full individual capability. It demonstrates that their manager knows about their work and their challenges and is supporting them in the delivery of the required outcome. It also lets the team member know that the manager is shouldering their ultimate accountability for the work output of their direct reports.

The outcome of good task assignment is:

- A common understanding of the task and the requirements of the manager and the team member.
- Strong team member engagement in the task.
- Successful task completion and outcome.
- A strong, two-way, trusting and productive working relationship based on achieving business goals together.
- Enhancement of the team member's capability.

A task assignment is not an assignment unless engagement occurs, otherwise it is a directive.

vi. Hold regular one-on-one meetings with every team member.

To ensure individual alignment and focus, every manager, at every level, needs to continually address the four basic questions that employees need answered to sustain high performance:

- Where are we going?
  (Local work plans. What are our priorities? What do we need to do to be successful?)
- What's my role?
  (What is my work? How does the change affect my role? How does it affect my pay? How does it affect my status?)
- How will my performance be measured/judged?
  (What does success look like?)
- Where am I going?
  (What is my future in the organization?) To be answered by the manager-once-removed.

By answering these questions, managers ensure team members are focused on the delivery of strategic objectives.

Cascading strategy is about the alignment and distribution of work. It is about ensuring engagement and clarity, with each person understanding where their organization, function or department is going, understanding their role in strategy delivery and understanding what good performance looks like.

Key Concepts

- Cascading the strategy involves moving work from a high level, down the organization, to those who do the work. It is a continual process of engaging employees in strategy delivery, breaking up complex work into less complex tasks, allocating them with appropriate accountability and authority and providing the necessary resources to complete the task.
- Cascading a strategy begins by educating those who must execute it. Communication supports

the cascading process by setting the context and purpose of the change. It is not about allocating work, it is about providing the big picture.

- Team member's manager-once-removed (MOR) integrates the work of their team of teams and ensure their managers collaborate constructively to achieve the plan of the business unit. They hold meetings with their immediate subordinate managers and their team members to communication how the function needs to work together to deliver the required outcomes.

- Every manager at every level reviews the initiatives they have been allocated and engages their team on strategy implementation. They discuss with their team *what* must be achieved and *why* it must be achieved.

- Managers align the work in their team by breaking down complex objectives or tasks into component tasks and allocating them to team members.

- When assigning tasks, managers ensure each task has the context, purpose, quality and quantity required. There must also be a clear understanding of the time the task is due and the resources are available for task completion (CPQQRT).

- For a strategy to be implemented effectively, every employee must know how they are expected to change, as well as what they are expected to deliver and how. Specifically, they must know:
  - ➢ Where are we going?
    (What is our direction? What are our priorities? What do we need to do to be successful?)
  - ➢ What's my role?
    (What is my part in this?)
  - ➢ How will my performance be measured/judged?
    (What will success look like?)

Tips for Getting Started

1. Review a goal or task that you have assigned as part of the performance planning process. Did it cover all aspects of the CPQQRT method? If not, how can you improve it?

2. If you are a manager of managers, hold a three-level meeting. Discuss current business performance or strategy issues. In the meeting, outline your expectations of how each team contributes and how their work integrates and enables you to achieve the functions objectives.

3. Review one of your goals that relate to strategy deployment:
   - How does it align with the goals of your manager?
   - How have you cascaded this goal to the performance plans of your team members?

4. For one of your strategic goals, answer for yourself:
   - Where are we heading (as a department, division or organization)?
   - What is my role?
   - How is my performance measured?

5. Hold a one-on-one meeting with each of your team members. Provide answers to the same questions in relation to their strategic goals:
   - Where are we heading (as a division or organization)?
   - What is their role?
   - How is their performance measured?

Additional information available at www.theleadershipframework.com.au

1. Understand your role.
2. Setting conditions for constructive working relationships.
3. What is work?

4. Creating effective roles and putting good people in them.
5. Effectively assigning and assessing work.
6. Develop team capability.
7. Build good teamwork.
8. Enabling continuous improvement and leading change.
9. Understanding resistance to change.
10. Change management action plan template.

Chapter 6

The Strategy Implementation Process – Monitoring and Assuring the Strategy

Systems for data collection, analysis and reporting, combined with effective strategy review meetings, strategy assessment meetings and an effective performance planning system, are essential for successful strategy implementation.

MONITORING AND ASSURING the strategy is the final step in strategy implementation. As well as developing a governance system to track and compare results against the strategic plan, monitoring and assuring includes reviewing planning assumptions and the allocation of resources. It also requires the balancing of short-term operational needs with long-term strategic priorities, which is a major management challenge for many organizations.

Monitoring & assuring the strategy

At the organizational level, monitoring and assuring strategy implementation is done as specific processes. At an individual level, it is done as part of the normal day-to-day work of managers.

Specific Processes to Monitor and Assure Strategy Implementation

i.   Systems for data collection, analysis and reporting.

To enable the effective monitoring of strategy implementation, the leadership team is accountable to develop appropriate data collection, analysis and reporting systems. While this is sometimes difficult, it often depends on how effectively the strategy was defined in the first place, i.e.

with clear objectives, specified initiatives with appropriate measures and targets (see Chapter 3: The Strategy Implementation Process – Defining the Strategy).

When these systems are well designed, with the right metrics at the right level, the focus will be on why problems occur and the corrective action required. If poorly designed, then the information collected may be of limited use.

Whether the data is good or not, the implementation of the strategy and related initiatives must still be assessed. As a minimum, tracking the deployment of approved resources can be a useful lead indicator of whether an initiative is being executed.

ii.   Strategy review meetings.

Operational review meetings and strategy review meetings are different and, as such, they should be separate meetings. Operational review meetings examine organizational, functional and departmental performance and address new or persistent problems. They address day-to-day operating problems, such as defects, bottlenecks, scheduling, supplier concerns, cash flow issues and sales performance.

Strategy review meetings discuss implementation of the strategy and its related initiatives. These meetings involve all members of the leadership team, with input from initiative owners and relevant managers with more specific functional expertise. Attendees conduct a high-level overview of strategy implementation. They assess the progress of strategy implementation and the causes and sources of implementation issues. They also recommend corrective actions and assign accountability to resolve issues. Often a separate strategy review meeting may be required for each objective as in-depth discussion is needed.

Holding separate operational and strategy review meetings avoids having short-term operational and tactical issues displace discussions of strategy implementation. While operational meetings are frequent, such as daily or weekly, strategy review meetings are typically monthly.

iii.   Strategy assessment meeting.

While poor strategy implementation has its own issues, so does implementing a wrong or an out-of-date strategy. A strategic plan is a set of hypotheses about cause and effect relationships. It is based on information and judgements made at a point in time. The business environment, however, is continually changing and judgements and assumptions can be wrong or outdated. Therefore, strategic plans need to be adaptable and flexible so they can respond to changes in both the internal and external environments. Therefore, the leadership team should put the whole strategy under full review at least once a year. This is done at a strategy assessment meeting.

Strategy assessment meetings are used to check the strategy against changes to both the external competitive environment and the current internal environment. Since the creation of the strategy there may have been changes in the competitive environment, such as actions by new competitors or changes in regulation impacting the business. Furthermore, the organization will have collected additional data from its monitoring and analysis.

The leadership team must test, validate or modify the hypotheses embedded in the strategy, i.e. Does the strategy remain valid in light of the new knowledge, information, opportunities and changes to the environment?

Furthermore, they need to assess if completion of approved initiatives will lead to the achievement of the strategy, as planned. If not, are additional initiatives required and/or is an initiative to be modified or canceled?

The purpose of strategy review meetings is not to track initiatives. It is to review and assess if the strategy is still valid and if the strategy will be achieved by the initiatives; and if not, determine corrective action.

Comparison of Strategic and Operational Meetings

	Type of meeting		
	Operational review	**Strategy review**	**Strategy assessment**
Purpose	To respond to short-term problems and promote continuous improvement.	To monitor and support strategy implementation.	To improve strategy or change strategy.
Focus	Identify and solve operational problems.	Strategy implementation.	Assess and adjust the strategy if required in line with changing circumstances both internal and external.
Information	Dashboard for key performance indicators and financial summaries.	Reports on strategic objectives, initiatives, measures and targets.	External and internal analysis, goal achievement and outcomes.
Frequency	Depends on business needs and business cycle. Usually daily, weekly or monthly.	Monthly or quarterly, depending on requirements.	Quarterly to annually, depending on the speed of the industry; also whenever there is significant change to the external environment that may impact the organization.
Attendees	Departmental and functional team members. The leadership team.	The senior leadership team. Those roles accountable for delivery of strategic objectives and initiatives.	The senior leadership team. Those roles accountable for delivery of strategic objectives and initiatives.

Adapted from *Mastering the Management System* by Robert S. Kaplan and David P. Norton. *Harvard Business Review*, January 2008.

Day-to-Day Processes to Monitor and Assure Strategy Implementation

The organization's strategy should normally be integrated into the performance planning process, as goals and tasks (see Chapter 5: The Strategy Implementation Process – Cascading and Deploying the Strategy). These are assessed as part of a manager's ongoing performance effectiveness reviews of team members, identifying any problems and impediments to achieving tasks. This is part of effective managerial leadership.

However, managerial leadership is more than just setting, monitoring and assessing team member's performance effectiveness. It is also about engaging team members in their work by continually addressing the four key questions that all employees can be expected to have. Keeping the focus on "the four questions" not only allows the manager to monitor progress, it engages each team member in their work and builds trust. These are:

1. Where are we going?
2. What's my role?
3. How will my performance be judged?
4. Where am I going?

These questions are often answered through the organization's systems of work; for example, "What is my role?" is contained in position descriptions, and "How will my performance be judged?" is in the performance appraisal system. Nevertheless, managers must continually set the context for team members and reinforce requirements through both formal and informal processes.

Key Concepts

- Monitoring and assuring the strategy is the final step in strategy implementation. At a high level this is done as a specific process. At another level, it is done as part of the normal day-to-day work of managers.

- To enable the effective monitoring of strategy implementation, the leadership team is accountable to develop appropriate data collection, analysis and reporting systems.

- A well-designed scorecard, with the right metrics, at the right level, captures not only outcomes, but also leading indicators for those outcomes.

- Strategy review meetings are used to discuss implementation of initiatives. Attendees conduct a high level overview of strategy implementation. They assess the progress of strategy delivery; whether the strategy is on track; and assess the causes of implementation problems. They recommend corrective actions and assign accountability for action.

- Strategy assessment meetings are used to test, validate and modify the hypotheses embedded in the strategy.

- Monitoring strategy implementation is also integrated into the performance planning process, as goals and tasks are assessed as part of every manager's ongoing performance effectiveness reviews, identifying any problems or impediments to achieving tasks.

- Managers must ensure team members are engaged in strategy implementation by continually addressing the four key questions that all employees can be expected to have.

- Without good governance processes, strategy implementation will be impaired.

Tips for Getting Started

1. Assess how effective your organization is in reviewing strategy implementation. How could you improve it?

2. Review the type of information used in your organization to monitor strategy implementation. Is it effective? Why? Why not?

Additional information available at www.theleadershipframework.com.au

1. Understand your role
2. What is work?
3. Creating effective roles and putting good people in them.
4. Effectively assigning and assessing work.
5. Build good teamwork.
6. Enabling continuous improvement and leading change.
7. Building constructive working relationships.

Chapter 7

Strategy Implementation and Structure

Leadership is embedded in an organization's structure and systems of work. Clearly defined roles, with appropriate accountabilities and authorities for work, are essential for strategy implementation.

A COMMON FAILURE in strategy implementation is a lack of leadership. As outlined in Chapter 4, leadership is not just about setting direction, leadership is also about creating a working environment that both enables and supports productive work. This is achieved by aligning the whole working organization, part of which is the organizations structure. Organizations that try to force a new strategy through an outdated or poorly designed structure, with poorly defined roles, will find their strategy implementation goes off track and may eventually stall.

Effective strategy implementation requires work to be organized and delegated to the right people, at the right level and in the right roles. These roles must be designed to work together, as roles tell people what they are supposed to do and what they are entitled to expect from others. Clear roles, with defined working relationships, provide the basic rules of engagement for people to work together. Basic rules such as: who needs to work with whom, who makes the decision and who carries out the work.

When looking at organizational design, the main issues for strategy implementation are:

- What work is to be grouped together and what work is to be separated?
- How many levels should the organization have?
- What roles are needed?
- How do we ensure everyone works together to deliver business outcomes?

Failure to address these questions may result in:

- Too many divisions or too many vertical levels of hierarchy.
- Blurred accountabilities and authorities for work.
- Duplication of effort.
- Work being performed by the wrong roles.
- Managers not adding value to the work of their direct reports.
- Too many meetings with little outcome.
- Micromanaging, which results in frustration and a lack of freedom to think.

All this impacts on the ability of people to work together and hinders strategy implementation.

Designing the Organization's Structure

The design of the organization's structure commences when the strategy to deliver the organization's purpose is clear. It is important to remember that while a transformational strategy may require a complete new structure, sometimes only minor adjustments to structure or roles may be required. The aim is to enable people to work together. Organizations that change structure just because they have a new strategy might disrupt something that works perfectly well.

The job of the CEO is to *organize* the work to be done. This involves grouping similar types of work together—the horizontal dimension; and organising work into different levels of complexity—the vertical dimension.

Dimensions of an organization's structure

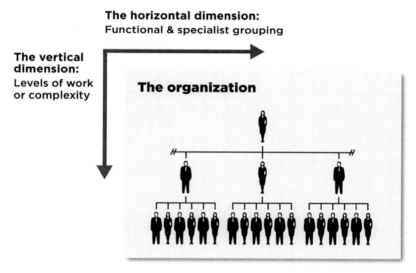

A map of our working relationships...

i. Designing the horizontal dimension.

In designing the horizontal structure, the issue is what work needs to be put together and what should be separated. In organizations, there are three broad types of functions:

- Core operational functions, such as production, sales and service.

- Specialist support/service functions, such as finance, human resources and information technology.
- Governance and control functions, such as audit.

The grouping and separation of work will vary from organization to organization, and each organization needs to make its own decision based on its strategy, size, complexity and business requirements. The source of structure issues, however, are often the same, i.e. issues of alignment and of clarity.

a) Aligning functions.

In the horizontal structure, issues often relate to accountability and authority and the allocation of resources. Unless this cross-functional work is properly aligned, silos will develop and workarounds may occur. Functions may start duplicating the work of other functions to achieve outcomes. Alternatively, no function will think they are accountable, so gaps in strategy implementation will occur, often resulting in accusation and conflict.

In strategy implementation, issues of accountability, authority and resourcing tend to be where work passes:

- From one function to the next, e.g. from the marketing division to the sales division.
- From head office to branches, where the latter is closer to the customer but the center sees the big picture. This is sometimes reflected on a larger scale, where global vs local organizations wrestle over pricing and marketing.
- From inside the organization to outsourced providers.

It is the role of the CEO to integrate the work of all functions by clearly defining where accountability and authority stops for one function and where it commences for the next.

A common problem for many organizations is the integration of the work of core functions and specialist corporate functions, such as finance, human resources and information technology. Typical issues are:

- What are the corporate specialist function vs core functions accountabilities and authorities for strategy development and implementation?
- How do corporate specialist functions integrate with line manager accountabilities and authorities?

Successful strategy implementation needs corporate specialist functions and core functions to work together. To enable this, their accountabilities and authorities must be aligned and be linked to the nature of their work.

Corporate specialist functions exist due to a need for specialist knowledge, skills and experience. Therefore, corporate specialist functions must be accountable to *develop* the organization's strategy for their area of expertise. The corporate specialist function must then *recommend* the specialist strategy to the CEO and leadership team. The authority to *decide* is performed by the CEO with input and feedback from the full leadership team.

Following this, it is logical that if a corporate specialist function is accountable to develop the specialist strategy, then they must also be accountable to *design* the systems of work to support the approved strategy.

When implementing corporate strategy, it is important to remember the role of the manager. The role of the manager is to *achieve the business goals set for them and, at the same time, provide an environment that allows their staff to be effective and satisfied with their work while developing their full potential* (see Chapter 9: Strategy Implementation and Effective Managerial Leadership).

For this reason, strategy implementation is led by each manager for their own team, in line with corporate requirements. The role of the corporate specialist function is to provide *advice* and *support* to the line manager in the performance of their role.

Lastly, as corporate specialist functions design the strategy and systems of work, it is logical they are also required to *monitor* and *audit* the implementation of the strategy.

The typical accountabilities and authorities for corporate specialist functions are outlined in the following table.

As can be seen from the table, line manager roles and corporate roles are complementary for strategy development and implementation. They are not in conflict. What is required is a clear understanding of the accountabilities and authorities of these complementary relationships.

Essential to this process is to embed the accountabilities and authorities for strategy development and approval, of ownership of systems of work and governance and control, in the organization's systems of work (see Chapter 8: Strategy Implementation and Systems of Work).

With a clear understanding of work requirements, organizations can design functions to support strategy implementation and not hinder it.

Typical Accountabilities and Authorities for Corporate Specialist Functions

Element	Corporate specialist functions (e.g. Safety, HR, Finance, IT)	Line manager roles CEO, executive team, managers
Strategy	• Develop and recommend the (specialist) strategy, e.g. IT Strategy, Finance strategy, HR Strategy, Safety Strategy, Communications Strategy *Typically uses advisory and coordinating authorities*	• Decide organization's strategy • Input to discipline strategy, e.g. IT, Finance, HR, Safety • Decide cross-functional strategies, e.g. IT, Finance, HR, Safety, Communications
System of work design	• Design and recommend the (specialist) system or process aligned with business strategy *Typically uses coordinating authorities*	• Input to the design • Decide the system
System of work use	Deliver service to enable managers to use the system in their own areas, for example: • Provide specialist services, e.g. recruitment, procurement • Provide training services • Provide advice on the use of the system • Coordinate activities to enable *Typically uses advisory, coordinating and monitoring authorities*	• Lead the implementation, using the system as authorized • Initiate services within the agreed context of the function or system • Review and assure performance to system (by own team) • Decide trade-offs within systems limits *Typically uses service-getting authorities*
Governance: control, monitor, audit	• Collate and analyze data on compliance and quality • Recommend improvements • Recommend corrective action • Report against measures • Action authorized system changes *Typically uses monitoring and audit authorities*	• Provide data for reporting • Provide feedback on system effectiveness • Decide corrective action • Implement corrective action in own teams • Decide system changes

These "authorities" are outlined in Summary of Specialist's Role Relationships later in this chapter.

b) Aligning roles.

While aligning functions in an organization is essential, so too is the alignment of each role. It is not up to individuals to "work out" or to "discover how" they are to work with other roles to achieve business outcomes. It is the accountability of each manager to integrate and align the work of their team, as managers are the ones who are accountable for the output and behavior of their team.

The alignment of specialist roles, such as technical specialists and planners, is particularly important. These roles exist to support managerial work. They support the line by providing expertise or specialist services. They are critical to the effectiveness of the working organization.

As shown in the diagram below, specialist roles are authorized to do specific work. In this example the "Planner" is authoristed to coordinate work.

Defining working relationships

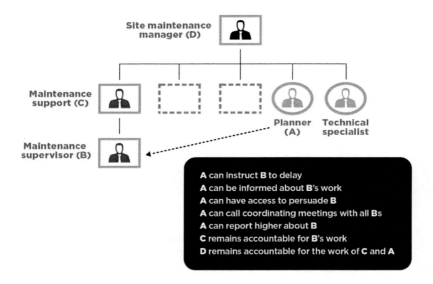

Site maintenance manager (D)

Maintenance support (C)

Planner (A)   Technical specialist

Maintenance supervisor (B)

A can instruct **B** to delay
A can be informed about **B**'s work
A can have access to persuade **B**
A can call coordinating meetings with all **B**s
A can report higher about **B**
C remains accountable for **B**'s work
D remains accountable for the work of **C** and **A**

Issues often arise when the specialist or other team members do not have a clear understanding of the nature of a specialist's separate, but complementary, work. It is therefore essential that organizations define the types of authority that can be used and what each authority means.

In organizations, there are six types of specialist role authorities. These are authorities to:

- Advise
- Get/Give service
- Monitor
- Coordinate
- Audit
- Prescribe

These authorities are summarized and compared in the following table, where A is the initiator and B is the responder.

Summary of Specialist's Role Relationships

Role components/ Accountabilities & authorities	Advisory	Service getting/ giving	Monitor	Coordinate	Audit	Prescribe
A can instruct B to do something	–	✓	–	–	–	✓
A can instruct B to stop & B stops	–	–	–	–	✓	✓
A can instruct B to delay & B delays	–	✓	✓	✓	✓	✓
A and B disagree. A decides	–	–	–	–	✓	✓
A can be informed about B's work	–	–	✓	✓	✓	✓
A can have access to persuade B	–	–	✓	✓	✓	✓
A can have access to explain to B	✓	–	✓	✓	✓	✓
A can call coordinative meeting with Bs	–	–	–	✓	–	–
A can report higher about B	–	✓	✓	✓	✓	✓
If A and B disagree, they do what their immediate manager would want	–	✓	–	✓	–	–

Note that the requirement for all employees to collaborate is defined in Chapter 9: Strategy Implementation and Effective Managerial Leadership.

To avoid conflict, it is essential that the accountabilities and authorities of each specialist are authorized and clear. These relationships must also be embedded into the organization's systems of work and communicated to the people whose roles are required to work together.

Failure to specify the accountabilities and authorities for specialist roles creates the environment for conflict and has predictable consequences:

- Office politics may emerge, with the related poor behaviors undermining the organization's effectiveness or corrupting its values.
- Time and resources will be wasted in "sorting out" the work.
- Workarounds and unauthorized systems of work will be developed as people will still want to achieve their objectives outside the authorized system of work.
- The specialist's manager will not be able to hold the specialist to account for their personal effectiveness because the specialist is likely to be trying to deal with ineffective working relationships and may not to have clear authority to act.
- Employees will need to rely on the goodwill of their peers to get work done.

Understanding, engaging with and respecting the role of specialists, with their legitimate accountabilities and authorities, allows roles (people) to work together to support strategy implementation.

ii. Designing the vertical dimension—creating levels of work.

Before looking at the vertical structure and strategy implementation, it is important to understand the nature of work in organizations. Only then can the number of vertical levels required and the type of work to be performed at each level be decided.

According to Dr. Elliott Jaques, work is a mental process. It might be associated with physical things, such as fabricating, repairs or digging a hole, but work is the internal mental processes that people use, quite naturally, to figure out problems in a task and solve them. It is in the *exercising of judgement* that people apply their intellect, their knowledge, skills and experience to a problem.

Jaques sees the vertical structure of an organization as a series of levels, where the *exercising of judgement in making decisions and acting on them* occurs at different levels of complexity and over distinctly different time frames. This complexity is created by a number of subjective and objective factors such as an increasing number of variables in a task, an increasing rate of change of variables, the increasing inter-dependence of multiple tasks, an increasing number of factors for the success and increasing ambiguity of feedback on the success of the task.

According to Jaques, each organizational level (or stratum) adds value in a different way; however, the type of work performed in each stratum is the same. The first three stratums in an organization (stratums I, II and III) are concerned with "doing" work. This work may consist of buying, selling, and/or providing services or products. This is where most of the organization operates: planning the work, implementing the work and executing the work.

The next two levels (stratums IV and V) move away from concrete activities of work to those which are more complex, often abstract, and represent progress by degrees over longer periods of time. These levels are the executive levels of the organization. It is where continuity of operations is maintained while the organization follows its strategic intent to a new desired future. The time from concept to completion is longer. For example, for the CEO of a stratum V level organization, the time from developing a strategy to being able to assess the success of the strategy will be five to ten years. The strategy may include developing new products or technologies or finding and developing new markets, including mergers and acquisitions.

The next two levels (stratum VI and VII) are that of multinational or international corporations and international bureaucracy. Here decisions are made on multinational and global issues of resource allocation, integrated profit and loss statements, and decisions where and in what to invest or divest and when and why. They are concerned with integrated thinking across diverse fields.

Due to their size, their nature and the complexity of their business, organizations will vary in the number of stratums required. However, unless the work is performed at the right level by the right people, outcomes will not be achieved. The only way to ensure this occurs is for the organization to be structured in the way that reflects the level of complexity for the required work. Therefore, a vertical level of management must only be created where the work is more complex than the work of the role below. This is so that, at each level, managers can add value to the roles immediately below them and that the right work is performed at the right level by the right people.

The following table provides an example of the types of work in a typical five-stratum organization.

Examples of Levels of Work

Stratum level	Time span	Type of work	Typical roles
V	**5–10 years** Immediate results are not available to verify results. The more complex decisions create a point of no return. Choices made can result in loss of value to shareholders.	**Develops strategy** Sets business direction and delivers the organization's purpose: *Ensures that an overall strategy is continually developed and refined to maximize the value that the organization delivers to stakeholders.*	• Managing director • CEO • Division of a multinational organization
IV	**2–5 years** Up to 5 years before the outcome of tasks can be assessed and before the benefits or otherwise are realized.	**Integrates the work** Executes strategy and improves systemsof work: *Designing system improvements to optimize long-term outcomes to maximize stakeholder value.*	• General managers • Vice presidents
III	**1–2 years** Up to 2 years before the most complex task can be completed and the fruits of the decision can be seen and judgement confirmed.	**Plans the work** Sustains operational delivery of function: *Ensuring that the key processes are under control to sustain delivery of outputs which contribute to the achievement of outcomes over time.*	• Managers of managers

(Continued)

Examples of Levels of Work *(Continued)*

Stratum level	Time span	Type of work	Typical roles
II	**3 months–1 year** Impacts of decisions can take up to 12 months to become apparent.	**Implements the work** Team leadership and process performance: *Manages trends and input consumption and control processes to achieve those outputs consistently.*	• Frontline manager • Lawyers • Accountants • HR professionals • Tax specialists
I	**1 day–3 months** Failures in judgement become apparent quickly. Outcome of actions can be more or less predicted with accuracy.	**Executes the work** Skilled production and output: *Completes tasks assigned and adheres to defined procedures. Monitors processes and reports on anomalies.*	• Operator level • Electrician • Manual laborer • Call center staff • Sales representative • Barista • Personal assistant

The reality is that organizations cannot function effectively if, as the result of poor organizational design, a level is missing, partially present or overlaps with other levels. If any of this occurs, there are predictable consequences:

- If there are too many levels, work will become too confined, with not enough room for decision making.
  - ➢ Managers will not add value to the work of their team as they will be operating at a similar level. Accountability becomes confused. Work will not be challenging or satisfying. More and more meetings will occur and it will not be clear who is accountable for the outcomes as authority is not clear.

> ➤ Managers will have a lack of freedom to think, with too many people checking and cross-checking work. This encourages micromanagement.
> ➤ Managers will build more and more processes and policies to control what is irrelevant. Organizational strategy will be lost as communication across the organization will become difficult. To overcome this, organizations often create or enhance communications departments to do what should be managerial work.

- If a role is compressed—that is, where a role operates at the same or similar level of complexity as a direct reporting role—the unique value add of the role will be unclear with overlap and duplication. Managers add value for their direct reports by solving problems, managing complexity and managing ambiguity at one level higher than their direct reports. When this does not happen:
  > ➤ Direct reports may skip a level in order to have issues resolved.
  > ➤ Authority and accountabilities will likely be blurred and fuzzy, yet everyone is really busy.
  > ➤ Internal politics will be intense and who is accountable for what will be an issue.
- If a work level is missing—that is, where manager positions operate at more than one level higher than their direct reports—there will be a lack of traction in getting action on strategies or plans.
  > ➤ Managers may not articulate concepts, strategy, goals and tasks at a level of detail that their direct reports can action. Objectives may be unclear as there is no context and little prioritization.
  > ➤ The managerial leader will often have to dip down to fill the missing work level, and this is unsatisfactory for all parties.

- If a role is stretched across multiple work levels, its unique value add will be confused or unclear. It is likely the role's authority will not match its accountabilities and it will be trying to deliver too much to too many. This will disempower direct reports and in turn will disempower the work levels below. It may result in bottlenecks, hasty or inappropriate decisions and changing priorities.

Ensuring vertical levels align to the different levels of complexity of work not only enables productive work, it supports strategy implementation.

Accountability for Organizational Design

The design and implementation of an organization's structure is a key accountability of the CEO; however, others also have a role.

i.   The board of directors and CEO.

The board, together with the CEO, define the purpose of the business so that value is delivered to customers and stakeholders. The board approves the strategy and then delegates the accountability (with appropriate authority) to the CEO to take the organization in the direction set to deliver the strategic objectives and to establish the conditions necessary to ensure effective delivery of value.

The CEO then sets the direction of the organization, aligned to the purpose. Based on this, the CEO applies managerial leadership to create an effective organizational structure by:

- Grouping similar work and deciding which core and corporate specialist functions are required, i.e. the first organizational units beneath and reporting to the CEO.

- Aligning the work of all functions so they can work together.
- Deciding the number and design of departments within each function, with recommendations from their direct reports.
- Deciding, with the board chair, the number of levels of management from the CEO role to the front line. This may vary for each function.

ii. The CEO and executive team.

The leadership team ensures a consistent approach is taken across the organization. They ensure that:

- A set of organizational design principles and practices is established to inform the design and deployment of structure in the organization—to design functions, departments and frontline output teams.
- All managers at all levels have a working understanding of the principles and guidelines.
- All managers understand their accountabilities and authorities in relation to design and deployment of structure.
- The whole organization and each of its parts have minimum, but sufficient, layers of management.
- The role of managers and team members in the organization are defined, clear and communicated (see Chapter 9: Strategy Implementation and Effective Managerial Leadership).

To support the above, the head of Human Resources, as the custodian of the organizational design system, provides advice, monitors and reports on all organizational and role design issues.

iii. Managers of managers.

Each manager of managers applies managerial leadership to align their team of teams, to ensure that planned work is delivered effectively. Specifically they:

- Integrate the work of their team of teams and ensure collaboration across their part of the organization.
- Decide on how many subordinate roles their managers will have and at what level these roles are positioned.
- Design roles—agree on the structure of the team below and ensure roles are appropriately placed for the complexity of work required.
- Monitor cross-organizational collaboration between their own part of the organization and other parts and work with their peers and their own immediate managers to ensure that cross-organizational work flows smoothly.

iv. Every manager at every level.

The role of the manager is to *achieve the business goals set for them and, at the same time, provide an environment that allows their staff to be effective and satisfied with their work while developing their full potential.* They are accountable to build and lead an effective team, so that each member is fully committed to and capable of moving in the established direction. Part of this is to recommend and implement approved structural changes.

Managers with specialist direct reports must:

- Ensure the specialist's role accountabilities and authorities are clear and that they are understood by their counterparts in the organization.
- Monitor the specialist's work, the quality of their collaboration with counterparts, provide meaningful feedback and coach for improved effectiveness.

- Identify early signs of conflict and act to resolve it productively.
- Collaborate with counterpart managers to resolve issues that cannot be resolved by the direct report.
- Ensure that their direct reports performance on collaboration and conflict resolution is reviewed as part of their performance review.

Line managers working with specialist roles must be clear on the specialist's accountabilities and authorities of those roles and respect them. If the accountabilities or authorities are not clear, then they must discuss this with the specialist's manager.

Key Concepts

- Leadership is about creating a working environment that both enables and supports productive work. A key component of this is good organizational design.
- An organization's structure provides the shared understanding of the working relationships that exist among people whose work must be aligned and integrated to deliver the organization's products and services.
- Good organizational design is more than just creating roles in a structure. It is about creating the right roles, with defined working relationships and with appropriate accountability authority.
- Clear roles with defined working relationships and appropriate accountability and authority provide the basic rules of engagement for people to work together—who needs to work with whom, who makes the decision and who carries it out.
- The design and implementation of an organization's structure is a key accountability of the CEO.

> ➤ The CEO and the leadership team must create a set of organizational design principles and practices to inform the design and deployment of structure and roles in the organization.
> ➤ All managers at all levels need to have a working understanding of these principles and guidelines.

- In designing the horizontal structure, the issue is what work needs to be put together and what should be separated. The grouping and separation of work will vary from organization to organization and each organization needs to make its own decision based on its strategy, size, complexity and business requirements.
- The location of work issues in the horizontal structure is usually at the handoff points between functions/ departments.
- The vertical structure in an organization is a series of levels where the exercising of judgement in making decisions and acting on them occurs, at different levels of complexity and over distinctly different time frames. Unless the work is performed at the right level by the right people, outcomes will not be achieved. The only way to ensure this occurs is for the organization to be structured in the way that reflects level of complexity for the required work.

Tips for Getting Started

1. Select a corporate function, such as Human Resource or Finance, in your organization. Using the table 'Typical Accountabilities and Authorities for Corporate Specialist Functions' in this chapter, assess if the accountabilities for strategy development, systems of work and governance are clear. Using this information, assess if core functions and specialist functions have been aligned and integrated. Discuss your findings with the relevant corporate function.

2. Using the table 'Examples of Levels of Work', assess if the type of work in your role is one level of complexity above your direct reporting roles. How do you know this?

Additional information available at www.theleadershipframework.com.au

1. The organizational design sequence.
2. Principles for organizational design.
3. Accountabilities and authorities for organizational design.
4. What is work?
5. Description of levels of work.
6. What is individual capability?
7. Matching accountability with authority
8. Creating effective roles and putting good people in them.

Chapter 8

Strategy Implementation and Systems of Work

Leadership is embedded in an organization's structure and systems of work. Effective systems of work are essential for successful strategy implementation.

AS PREVIOUSLY STATED, leadership is not just about setting direction, leadership is also about creating a working environment that both enables and supports productive work. This is achieved by aligning the whole working organization, part of which is the organization's systems of work. Systems of work (i.e. the organization's policies, procedures, forms, information and communication technologies) are a key component of the working organization as they coordinate and direct the work of the organization's people to deliver its products and services.

Systems of work:

- Facilitate work across functions, across teams and within teams.

- Provide the *standardising* methods and boundaries for work.
- Align people and work with legislation, social norms and the organization's values.
- Allow the leadership team to monitor and verify that the organization's purpose and strategy are being achieved in accordance with its cultural, ethical and moral standards.

As part of the working organization, systems of work critically influence the ability of people to do their best work. When well designed and aligned with requisite managerial leadership, their influence on people is highly positive. If, however, a system of work is poorly designed, it will be counter-productive, may not be used or may be misused. This not only impacts work outputs, it also hinders strategy implementation. This occurs where:

- The system does not do what it is supposed to do.
- Incorrect or incomplete inputs are received from others that delay or impair work.
- Accountabilities and authorities for the system or within the system are unclear.
- Handover points are not clear.
- The work outputs are not used or not trusted.

Therefore, it is a requirement that, as part of organizational alignment, all systems of work are designed to support strategy implementation (see Chapter 4: The Strategy Implementation Process – Aligning the Organization for Strategy Deployment).

Key Systems of Work for Strategy Implementation

While all systems of work need regular review, prioritizing the review, design and deployment of a system of work should be based on an organization's strategic requirements, i.e. systems of work that are key to strategy implementation should be reviewed first.

For example:

- A strategy to increase sales by improving customer satisfaction may need to implement an initiative to improve or replace the customer management systems, with the aim of speeding up service delivery or to improve the accuracy of a billing system to reduce customer complaints.
- A strategy to reduce costs may require an initiative to improve the procurement of goods and services. These initiatives could include prioritizing the review of processes to research procurement options, develop a procurement strategy, develop procurement documents, invite responses, evaluate responses, form a contract or to manage delivery.

There are, however, four systems that organizations must get right for successful strategy implementation. These are:

- The System of Systems
- The Strategy Implementation System
- The Organizational Design System (see Chapter 7: Strategy Implementation and Structure)
- The People Management Systems (see Chapter 9: Strategy Implementation and Effective Managerial Leadership)

The System of Systems

To improve their systems of work, organizations often go straight to total quality management systems, lean management or Six Sigma programs. In doing this they fail to look at the high level issues causing problems, such as lack of leadership, poor organizational alignment or proper processes for the design and review of systems of work. While these tools provide great opportunity for improvement, before doing so, organizations should ensure that all systems are authorized and productive for the purpose they are designed, as there is little point in making an ineffective system more efficient.

A System of Systems defines the methodology, accountabilities and authorities for the review, design and deployment of an organization's systems of work. It ensures that the accountabilities and authorities for work are in the right place, linked to the organization's authorized structure and that the system delivers the outcomes required.

All systems of work must conform to defined essential design principles. Only when this is done should organizations use other process improvement tools.

a) Design principles for a System of Systems.

As a minimum, a System of Systems must include the following eight design principles:

1. All systems of work must have a designated system owner.

Every system of work must have a designated owner of the system. For any system of work, this is the cross-over manager for all users of the system. This is because the cross-over manager is the only role that:

- Can work across all related processes within the system, with the authority and experience to identify and implement necessary changes.
- Has the authority to engage the whole team to understand and agree on the principles of the system, to assure it is fit for use and then to hold them accountable for input, implementation, and review.
- Can understand and integrate all the feedback loops and time delayed effects in the system.

- Can ensure the system of work is used effectively across the whole area of application.

Having the cross-over manager as the systems owner ensures the whole system is considered when it is designed or when changes are made. In this way, decisions can be made on what is best for the total system of work, not just to satisfy a person or department.

2. **All systems of work must be designed to meet the needs of the customer, end user, or beneficiary of the system.**

As systems exist to deliver specified outputs for customers, end users, or beneficiaries of the system of work, these people/roles must be identified and their needs understood and specified. This is important so that:

- The quality, quantity and timeliness of system outputs can be determined.
- Stakeholders can be advised or consulted when the system is altered or is to cease operation.

3. **All systems of work must be consistent with legislation, regulation and other corporate policies and standards.**

All systems must be consistent with legislation, regulation and the other corporate policies that reflect the organization's standards and values. For example, the development of a sales or production system must be consistent with other relevant organizational systems, such as the People Management System, Safety Management System, Environmental and Quality Management Systems. Failure to do so would not only put the organization at risk, it would be inconsistent with organizational requirements and would inevitably lead to conflict with those who work in other systems of work.

4. The design of all systems of work must include the specification of working relationships.

Working relationships must be established between roles, not people (see Chapter 7: Strategy Implementation and Structure). Establishing clear role relationships enables work to be done and disagreements to be resolved. In establishing working relationships, the systems designer must specify the accountabilities and authorities for each role that uses the system of work. This will ensure clarity on issues around the systems inputs, processes, outputs and feedback mechanisms.

5. All stakeholders must be engaged in the development and use of the system.

All the system's stakeholders must be consulted on its development and use. Where required, a user reference group can be created to provide input. This will not only ensure appropriate input and an appropriate level of consultation in the systems design, it will also build trust and reduce the potential for conflict in the future.

6. All systems of work must equalize treatment of employees, unless there is a business-related reason not to equalize.

When looking at different systems of work, it is important to understand their intent. Is the intent to differentiate or to equalize? Systems of equalisation treat people the same way. They do not differentiate between an operator, manager or the CEO. An example of this is a safety system. Irrespective of your position, title or rank, if you enter certain work sites, you must wear a hard hat and other required personal protective equipment. Systems that equalize promote organizational trust and fairness.

Systems of differentiation treat people differently. They distinguish between roles. For example, some roles may be paid based on commissions, while others are not.

All systems of work should equalize unless there is a clear work-related or business-related reason not to. If there is no such reason for a system that differentiates, the system and the managerial work associated is likely to be seen by employees to be unfair and can be expected to diminish mutual trust in the organization. Unfair systems drive non-compliance and dysfunctional behavior.

7. All systems of work must have evaluation and control built into the system design.

Systems can only be maintained as authorized and productive systems if control and audit work is effectively established. Controls assure the correct use of the system.

Where possible, measures must also be established. These measures must be directly related to the purpose and outcomes of the system. They need to consider all aspects of the output: quality, quantity, cost, and timeliness.

Example of Controls and Measures for a Recruitment System

Control	Measure	Period
Example 1: Recruitment. Quarterly dashboard (internal)	Cost per hire *(cost)* Time to fill *(timeliness)*	Post-recruitment review Quarterly report
Example 2: Recruitment. End of probation questionnaire manager (internal)	Quality of hire against position description and key values/ behaviors *(quality)*	3 months after hire (end of probation)

8. All systems of work must have a continuous improvement process built into the system design.

All systems of work must be designed with feedback mechanisms. The system's owner/custodian is accountable to ensure suggestions are considered and changes authorized and communicated.

Using these design principles will not only support strategy implementation, it will improve productivity, improve organizational trust, the quality of the working environment and reduce unnecessary conflict.

b.   Accountability for a System of Systems.

Designing effective systems is complex work. It requires an understanding of the organization's purpose, strategic objectives, the internal and external environment and their impacts on the business. It also requires the ability to ensure that each system of work produces the required outcomes for the business, in a way that is in line with the organization's values. This is high-level work.

Unfortunately, in most organizations, the design and deployment of systems of work has been moved to lower levels in organizations or leadership has been transferred to IT departments. Neither case is appropriate as accountability and authority for system design and deployment needs to be with the system owner.

It is the accountability of the CEO and the leadership team to provide effective systems of work. Therefore, they are also accountable to ensure the organization has a standard method for the design, deployment and review of systems of work.

The key roles, critical to the success of a System of Systems, are outlined in the table below.

Key Roles in a System of Systems

Role	Description
1. System owner*	This is the only position that is authorized to implement or significantly change the system, not merely propose changes.
	Where a system crosses departments, the system owner will be the cross-over manager for all departments that use the system (not normally below a stratum level III manager and usually a general manager/VP– stratum IV).
	The cross-over manager for organization-wide systems it is the CEO.

(Continued)

Key Roles in a System of Systems *(Continued)*

Role	Description
2. System custodian*	The position of the person who is accountable for monitoring the application of the system and advising the owner of the outcome. Usually holds accountability to undertake the work.
	For organization-wide systems it is a general manager/VP. Generally, the system custodian will gather input for the purpose of formulating a recommendation to the system owner. This may require the use of systems designers or reference groups.
3. System designer* and system design team	The position of the person who designs or redesigns the system. May be the system owner, custodian or delegated by the custodian (never below a stratum level III role).
4. Systems reference group member	Employees (including managers) representing key areas affected by the system of work. They are selected to advise the system designer or systems design team on issues relating to the application of the system.
5. Systems implementers	All managers whose teams are affected by the system of work are accountable for implementing the system in their team.
6. Systems users	All users of the system of work.
7. Systems auditor	May be an internal or external nominated role, independent to the system owner/custodian.

* The system owner, custodian and designer may be the same role, or the owner may agree with the custodian to delegate some elements to other roles. The owner retains full accountability for the system of work.

It should be noted that in a System of Systems, as managers are accountable for the output and behavior of their team, all managers at all levels are accountable to:

- Effectively implement authorized systems of work in their area.
- Discuss with their team how to specifically apply the system in a work area.

- Ensure the appropriate use of those systems of work in their area.
- Provide feedback to the system owner/custodian on the effectiveness of the system of work (using the system's feedback mechanisms).
- Monitor to ensure the system of work is being used as intended in their area.

Managers are not authorized to change the system of work without approval from the system owner/custodian.

All employees are accountable to:

- Work within set systems of work and refer issues to a higher level where appropriate.
- Look at ways to improve by providing feedback to their manager on the systems of work used.

Individual employees are not authorized to change a system of work without the approval of their manager.

It is only by having an effective System of Systems that organizations can ensure all other systems operate as planned and support strategy implementation.

The Strategy Implementation System

The Strategy Implementation System ensures the delivery of strategic objectives. It contains policies, procedures, forms, information and communication technologies necessary for strategy delivery. To be effective, the Strategy Implementation System must reflect the four steps of the Strategy Implementation Process. These are to:

1. **Define the strategy:** Clarify strategic objectives and their related initiatives so they can be implemented (see Chapter 3: The Strategy Implementation Process - Defining the Strategy).

2. **Align the organization:** Get ready for deployment by aligning the working organization for strategy implementation, connecting planning and budgeting, and allocating accountability and authority at a high level (see Chapter 4: The Strategy Implementation Process – Aligning the Organization for Strategy Deployment).

3. **Cascade work:** Engage all employees and assign tasks with appropriate measures and targets (see Chapter 5: The Strategy Implementation Process – Cascading and Deploying Strategy).

4. **Monitor and assure strategy delivery** (see Chapter 6: The Strategy Implementation Process – Monitoring and Assuring Strategy Implementation).

The Strategy Implementation System must also reflect that different types of work need to be performed at different levels of the organization.

Complexity, time span & organizational work

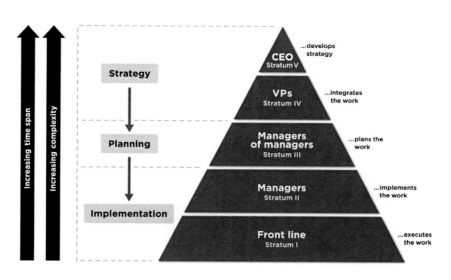

Using an example of a five-level organization (see diagram above), the five levels of work are organized into three broad categories:

1. **Strategy development:** Those who develop the strategy and integrate the work to delivery it—stratums IV and V.
2. **Planning the work:** Those who plan the work—stratum level III.
3. **Implementing or doing the work:** Those who implement the work and execute it—stratums I and II.

Therefore, in this example, the accountabilities for strategy implementation, aligned to the five levels of work are:

1. The board and CEO.

The board, together with the CEO, define and communicate the purpose of the business so that value is delivered to customers and stakeholders. The CEO then sets the direction of the organization, aligned to the purpose, and new strategy, and establishes conditions to ensure the effective delivery of value.

2. The CEO and leadership team.

The CEO and the leadership team (VPs/general managers) contributes to the board's direction, in a five-year timeframe, and develops the strategic initiatives to move the organization in the direction set (by the CEO). To do this they:

- Set strategic measures and targets.
- Align the organizational structure and systems of work.
- Initiate systems to monitor and assure strategic initiatives.
- Authorize spending for the implementation, which may, depending on the value of this spending, require approval from the board.
- Create effective managerial leadership processes.

3. Managers of managers at all levels.

As cross-over managers, they anchor the work and take the necessary action to ensure the delivery of the strategic objectives and their related initiatives. Managers of managers are accountable to integrate and align the work of their team of teams. Specifically they:

- Ensure the organizational structure is effective for the work required.
- Establish systems of work that integrate the end-to-end processes of the business unit.
- Apply managerial leadership to align departments in an effective manner.
- Decide on how many subordinate roles their managers will have and at what level these roles are positioned.
- Agree on the structure and roles of the team below, and ensure roles are appropriately placed for the complexity of work required with defined working relationships to enable collaboration.
- Ensure the objectives, roles, accountabilities and authorities for all parties are clear.
- Set the context and direction of the business unit.
- Monitor cross-organizational collaboration between their own part of the organization and other parts and work with their peers and their own immediate manager to ensure that cross-organizational work flows smoothly.
- Provide the necessary resources to deliver initiatives.

4. Managers at every level.

Managers are accountable *to achieve the business goals set for them and, at the same time, provide an environment that allows their staff to be effective and satisfied with their work while developing their full potential.* In relation to strategy delivery, this means that managers at every level must:

- Set the purpose and direction for their team.
- Build and lead an effective team so that each member is fully committed to and capable of moving in the direction set.
- When the direction or a system of work changes, they are accountable to lead change in their team.
- Continually provide context for the team and for each individual team member. This means addressing four key concerns that team members can be expected to have:
  - ➢ Where are we going?
  - ➢ What is my role?
  - ➢ How is my performance measured?
  - ➢ What is my future? (To be answered by the manager-once-removed.)

5. Team member (employee) accountability.

Every employee at every level must:

- Fulfil commitments made.
- Bring their full capability to work.
- Continue to develop their performance effectiveness.
- Provide their manager with feedback.
- Work together productively.

It is only when every employee at every level understands and delivers their accountabilities for strategy implementation that the organization's strategic initiatives will be effectively implemented.

Key Concepts

- Leadership is about creating a working environment that both enables and supports productive work. A key component of this is effective systems of work.

- A system of work is a framework that ensures a replicable set of activities are performed to achieve a specific business purpose in line with the organization's values. They include a set of interacting and interrelated elements, such as policies, procedures, forms, information and communication technologies.
- Systems of work:
  - ➢ Facilitate work across functions, across teams and within teams.
  - ➢ Provide the standardising methods and boundaries for work to be done.
  - ➢ Align people and work with legislation, social norms and the organization's values.
  - ➢ Allow the leadership team to monitor and verify that the organization's purpose and strategy are being achieved in accordance with its cultural, ethical and moral standards.
  - ➢ Systems of work critically influence the ability of people to do their best work.
- Where systems of work are well designed, and aligned with requisite managerial leadership, their influence will be highly productive. If poorly designed, not used or misused, their influence will be counter-productive and can cause conflict.
- To ensure all systems of work produce the required outcomes, they must conform to defined essential design principles. As a minimum, all systems of work must:
  - ➢ Have a designated system owner.
  - ➢ Be designed to meet the needs of the customer, end user, or beneficiary of the system.
  - ➢ Be consistent with legislation, regulation and other corporate policies and standards.
  - ➢ Specify working relationships in the system of work.

- ➢ Engage all stakeholders on the development and use of the system.
- ➢ Equalize the treatment of employees unless there is a business reason not to equalize.
- ➢ Have evaluation and control built into the system design.
- ➢ Have a continuous improvement process built into the system design.
- Prioritizing the review, design and deployment of a system of work should be based on the organization's strategic requirements, i.e. what systems of work are key to strategy delivery.
- Four systems that organizations must get right for successful strategy implementation are:
  - ➢ The System of Systems
  - ➢ The Strategy Implementation System
  - ➢ The Organizational Design System
  - ➢ The People Management System
- Designing effective systems is complex work. It requires an understanding of the organization's purpose and objectives and the external and internal impacts on the business. It also requires the ability to integrate what the organization values.
- Providing effective systems of work is a key accountability of the CEO and the executive team.
- All managers are accountable to:
  - ➢ Implement authorized systems of work in their area.
  - ➢ Discuss with their team the application of each system in their work area.
  - ➢ Ensure the appropriate use of systems of work in their area.
  - ➢ Provide feedback to the system owner/custodian on the effectiveness of the system of work (using the systems feedback mechanisms).
  - ➢ Monitor to ensure the system of work is used as intended.

- All employees are accountable to:
  - ➢ Work within set systems of work and refer issues to a higher level where appropriate.
  - ➢ Look at ways to improve systems of work by providing feedback to their manager.

Tips for Getting Started

1. Pick a system of work in your area. How do you know the process is operating effectively? What are the measures? What are the feedback mechanisms for the system of work?
2. Pick a system of work in your area and complete a systems scan. Identify areas for improvement. Note: a *system of work effectiveness scan* is available as a free download on The Leadership Framework website.
3. Review your organization's system of work for strategy implementation. Does it follow the process of defining the strategy, aligning the organization, cascading work and monitoring and assurance of strategy delivery? If not, determine how can the process be improved.

Additional information available at www.theleadershipframework.com.au

1. Systems of work and culture.
2. Systems of work—roles, accountabilities, and authorities.
3. Principles for design of a system of work.
4. Process for designing or reviewing a system of work.
5. Systems of work control document—template.
6. Example: System of work control document—People Management System.
7. Systems of work effectiveness scan.

Chapter 9

Strategy Implementation and Effective Managerial Leadership

The role of the manager is to achieve the business goals set for them. To do this they must provide an environment that allows their team to be effective and satisfied with their work, while developing their full potential.

CRITICAL TO SUCCESSFUL strategy implementation is the role of the manager. Managers not only design and deploy the organization's structure and systems of work, they are both part of and are impacted by the working organization. To perform their role, managers must have a coherent and integrated framework for managerial leadership. Without such a framework, they will not have the theoretical or practical base for what they must know, do or how to do it. This can result in an inappropriate focus on team member performance rather than the working organization, leading to poor manager-team member working relationships and a failure in outcomes.

A holistic and integrated framework for managerial leadership provides managers with:

- Clarity on the requirements of their role.
- Clear accountabilities and authorities for their people work.
- An understanding of how work is created and deployed.
- An understanding of impacts on team performance and individual effectiveness.
- Principles and practices to manage effectively and in a manner that builds trust.
- Methods and tools to improve team performance and to execute business unit strategy.
- A foundation for effective decision making.
- A checkpoint against which they can assess themselves.

For organizations, a holistic and integrated managerial leadership framework will:

- Provide consistency in leadership practices.
- Provide a common language to solve people management issues.
- Support cross-organizational alignment and productive working relationships between operational roles and specialist functions, such as finance and human resources.
- Provide managers with skills and tools to execute organizational strategy.
- Build an organizational culture consistent with the organization's values.

Providing such a framework is a key accountability of the CEO—just as the CEO's accountable for providing frameworks for financial management or procurement.

The Manager-Team Member Working Relationship

A critical but often neglected part of organizational design is the working relationship between managers and their team members. The design of these roles is critical as:

- Every team member (employee) reports to a manager.
- Every manager is the member of a team.
- Like any relationship, the manager and team member working relationship holds expectations by both parties. This applies equally to the CEO and their direct reporting team and frontline managers with their team.

It is only through design that the strong, two-way manager-team member working relationship, which is required for productive work, can be developed consistently throughout an organization.

This book uses the concepts, principles and practices of The Leadership Framework as the basis for strategy implementation and managerial leadership (see Appendix 1).

Designing the Manager Role

The role of a manager is more than the stewardship of a function. It is about setting direction and making decisions. It is about leading a team and creating the conditions for productive work. It is about defining and communicating the organization's unique position.

The role of a manager is to *achieve the business goals set for them and, at the same time, provide an environment that allows their staff to be effective and satisfied with their work while developing their full potential*. To do this, managers are specifically accountable for:

- The output and behavior of their team.
- Building and leading an effective team, so that each member is fully committed to and capable of moving in the established direction.
- Continuous improvement of work processes and methods.

This brings together several concepts with which organizations (and managers) often struggle.

- Managers are accountable for *the output and behavior of their team*. While all employees are accountable to deliver their work, managers are additionally accountable for the work outputs and behaviors of their direct reports.
- Managers are accountable for *building and leading an effective team so that each team member is fully committed and capable of moving in the direction set*. Managers set the purpose and direction of their team and enable team members to move along together in that direction with competence, commitment and enthusiasm, dealing with obstacles on the way. To do this, managers must build the capability of their team to achieve the required outputs. They must ensure that the working organization supports their team's work.
- In addition to the execution of the day-to-day operational work, managers are accountable for continuous *improvement of work processes and methods*. They identify ways for work to be done more effectively and efficiently. They then implement the necessary changes for this to occur.
- Every manager at every level is a leader of their team. As managers are accountable for the output and behavior of their team; for building and leading an effective team so that each member is fully committed to and capable of moving in the direction set; and for bringing about change through continuous improvement of work processes in their team, they must be leaders. Leadership is defined as: "The process in which one person sets the direction for one or more other people and gets them to move together in that direction with full commitment." Leadership is a specific accountability of all people managers, it is not

a freestanding activity, it is part of the role. Trying to separate leadership from management confuses the benefits of good managerial practice. All managers must be leaders. Their only choice is to be a good one or a bad one. On the other hand, not all leaders are managers.

To perform their accountabilities, managers must effectively deliver the performance management sequence. This sequence starts with effective role design, followed by selection for the role. It continues while the individual is working in the role. Each part of the process has a different emphasis with the same goal: having fully loaded roles filled with people capable of doing their work and achieving team outcomes.

This sequence is shown in the diagram below.

**The performance
management sequence**

- **Role design** establishes the role in the organization. It sets out its business reason, its purpose and objectives, its accountabilities and authorities, and its working relationships with other roles.
- **Selection** identifies and appoints an individual whose capability is judged to best suit the capability requirements of the role.

- **Induction** familiarizes those selected with the work of the role; its relationships with other roles and the incumbents in those roles; the systems of work, including the policies and work processes relating to the role; an overview of the typical tasks; the current priority tasks of the role; and the performance requirements of the role.
- **Assigning and assessing work** is a foundation condition for individual performance effectiveness. The manager then monitors the individual as they progress in the work, providing feedback about progress and how effectively the individual is working.
- **Reward** and recognize team members, as appropriate. The intent is to create conditions where all employees can see that the organization is a meritocracy—a place where people are paid fairly based on their performance effectiveness.
- **Development** in the role follows naturally from effective task assignment and completion, as the manager reviews the work and the individual's effectiveness in executing the work. The manager creates opportunities to coach the individual on how to be more effective. This may involve helping individual's see better ways to solve problems, run meetings, collaborate with others, comply with rules and policies, or better use the company's resources.

Having established what managers are to be held accountable to do and how they do it, role design is not complete without deciding on the authorities required to perform those accountabilities. Authorities are those aspects of a role that enable the person to act legitimately to carry out the accountabilities required of a role. Authorities include such things as authority to assign tasks, get access to information and expend resources.

To fulfil their accountabilities the manager role must be provided with two types of authorities:

- Work authorities.
- Role authorities (managerial).

i.   Work authorities.

These are the authorities required to do specific types of work, such as the technical and programming aspects of their role. This includes authorities to do specific tasks and to spend money. These authorities are usually specified in most organizations through position descriptions and delegation manuals.

ii.   Role authorities (managerial).

The second type of authority a manager must have is the authority stemming from their role as a people manager. To be held accountable for the work of their team, managers must be provided with four minimum role authorities. These authorities are to:

- Veto the appointment of a person to their team, with good reason.
- Assign tasks to team members.
- Review, recognize and reward performance differentially.
- Initiate the removal of poor performers from the role, with good reason and due process.

Note that these authorities must be exercised within the boundaries of the organization's policies, procedures and values.

So why do managers need these role authorities? Without these authorities, a manager will not be seen as the true leader and will have difficulty carrying out their accountability for achieving their output. If a manager is held to account for the output and behavior of their direct-reports, then it makes sense that the manager must be able to decide on the capability fit of a person to their team. If a person is to be transferred to their team, the manager must be able to veto the appointment to the team if they feel that it will adversely impact team performance.

If the manager is accountable for the output of the team, then they must be able to *assign tasks* to team members. In fact, the manager is the only person who can assign tasks to members of their team. If others are able to assign tasks, the manager will be unable to manage workloads effectively or ensure critical issues are addressed in balancing the work to be done. This is likely to impact upon others in the team. This does not mean that the manager's team members do not work with others; they do and must do for the organization to be successful. But it does mean all working relationships must be clear (as outlined in Chapter 7: Strategy Implementation and Structure).

Following this, as the manager assigns a task, it makes sense that they are the only person who can effectively judge or assess the performance of that task (*review*) and make fair judgments to *recognize* and *reward* team members based on those judgments (within the boundaries of the remuneration system). This is a most important authority, as it goes directly to an individual's sense of worth, and is therefore an important building block in the relationship between the manager and team member and is key to building trust.

The *initiate removal* authority is exercised when a team member is unable to deliver the required output for the role. The manager will have worked with the team member to identify the issues and, where appropriate, to develop and implement a performance improvement plan. If the team member's performance does not improve and the manager assesses the issues related to an incorrect fit to the role, then the manager is accountable to use this authority to remove the team member from the current role.

This authority is only to initiate removal from the team, as the manager should not have the authority to remove the person from the organization (dismissing the person). This authority rests with the employee's manager-once-removed (MOR), as it may be that the manager is underutilising that team member or not managing effectively. It may also be that the person's performance is related to long-standing and unresolved conflict. If placed in another role more suited to their skills, that person may thrive.

The interrelationship between manager accountabilities and authorities and the manager-once-removed is shown in the following table.

Accountabilities and Authorities of Managers and Managers-Once-Removed

	Manager	Manager-once-removed
Veto appointment	D	D
Induct and set context	D	–
Set type of task	D	–
Assign tasks	D	–
Coach and train for current role	D	–
Modify tasks	D	–
Expand and reduce task type	D	–
Recognize (verbal appraisal)	D	–
Review performance	D	–
Reward	D	–
Initiate removal from team	D	–
Dismiss	R	D
Assess career potential	R	D
Adjust pay band	R	D
Transfer	R	D
Promote/Demote	R	D
Judge an appeal	–	D

Adapted from Dr Elliott Jaques   R = Recommends, D = Decides

Designing the Team Member Role

The other part of the manager-team member working relationships is that of the team member. In addition to the technical and programing aspects of their role, all team members are accountable to work effectively with their manager, other team members and others in the organization. To do this, team members, at all levels, have five accountabilities to their manager. These accountabilities are:

- Fulfil commitments made.
  - ➢ Deliver in full and on time all their output commitments and expect the same of others. This includes commitments made across the organization to other individuals or departments.
  - ➢ Uphold the organization's values.
  - ➢ Under no circumstances should they "surprise" their manager on the delivery of output commitments.
- Bring their full capability to work.
  - ➢ Apply their knowledge, skills and experience fully and effectively.
  - ➢ Exercise their discretion to deliver outcomes fully and appropriately.
  - ➢ Try different ways to achieve objectives, even in difficult circumstances.
  - ➢ Work cooperatively with others to solve problems and share information within the context of the role.
  - ➢ Work within set policies, systems and procedures and refer to a higher level, where appropriate.
  - ➢ Accept and adapt to change.
- Continue to develop their performance effectiveness.
  - ➢ Work to improve their personal effectiveness in their role by actively participating in people management processes, such as goal-setting and development.
- Provide their manager with feedback.

- ➢ Actively engage with their manager when tasks are assigned.
- ➢ Look at ways to improve by providing feedback to their manager on tasks, systems and processes used.
- ➢ Refer problems that cannot be resolved to their manager for assistance.
- ➢ Immediately notify their manager if they are unable to achieve assigned task output (quantity, quality, time or cost).
- Work together productively.
  - ➢ Work together to solve problems within the context set by their manager.
  - ➢ Persuade each other to act in a way that facilitates their work, to accommodate each other's needs as far as possible without changing or compromising their accountabilities or agreed/allocated objectives.
  - ➢ Do what is right for the function and the organization, even when this may cause a potential difficulty for their area.
  - ➢ If there is disagreement, they act as their manager would want them to, before escalating to their manager.
  - ➢ If agreement cannot be reached, they must escalate to their immediate manager who will either clarify the context or make a specific trade-off decision.

The design of the manager and team member working relationships is critical for strategy implementation. It is only when every manager at every level and every team member at every level understands and delivers their accountabilities that the organization's strategic initiatives can be achieved.

People Management Systems

Managerial leadership needs to be supported by an effective People Management System. The People Management System includes processes to develop the organizational structure, create roles, select and induct new employees, assign and assess work, reward and develop people and provide fair treatment. While the whole People Management System is important for effective managerial leadership, several areas typically come into play for strategy implementation. These are the reward system and the talent systems. These are the systems that influence the attraction, retention and development of organizational capability.

a) Reward systems.

To attract and retain talent, people need to be paid appropriately. In relation to reward systems, the key issues are fair pay and differential pay.

i. Fair pay.

People have an inherent sense of what relative pay levels are fair. Those paid at equitable levels feel satisfied. Those paid below this feel exploited. People paid above this often feel insecure. In relation to pay the question is not necessarily "How much?" but "Is it fair?"

So what is an equitable level of pay? When making comparisons on pay, people ask three questions:

- How am I paid compared to others who do my job in other organizations? (external equity)

This comparison focuses on what employees in other organizations are paid for doing the same or similar roles. The fact that management views its employees as well paid compared with those of other organizations does not necessarily translate into employee beliefs. Employees have different information and make different comparisons than management.

- How am I paid compared to others at the same or higher levels in the organization? (internal equity)

This comparison focuses on what employees within the same organization, but with different roles, are paid. Employees make comparisons with lower level roles, roles at the same level (but with different skill requirements) and roles at higher levels. Internal equity is achieved when the pay structure is differentiated primarily by the level of work of the role, i.e. the role's complexity.

In his research, Elliott Jaques found that people's innate sense of fairness is aligned to a role's complexity as measured by the time span of the longest task, i.e. the length of time it took to carry out a role's longest-running assignment. For example, a maintenance worker in a factory might finish all tasks in 24 hours, but a purchasing manager may take three months to finalize a contract. A general manager/ vice president may take three to five years to plan and implement a new people management strategy. The longer the time span, the greater the complexity of the work, the greater amount of "felt fair pay" was appropriate to earn. This aligned with his work on an organization's levels of work or stratums.

The outcome of this research, i.e. the amount of relative pay that was "felt fair", is shown in the following table.

Stratum level	Time span	Relative pay	Salary example (rounded)
Stratum VII	20 years	16x	$2,400,000
Stratum VI	10–20 years	8x	$1,200,000
Stratum V	5–10 years	4x	$600,000
Stratum IV	2–5years	2x	$300,000
Stratum III	1–2 years	x	$150,000
Stratum II	3 months–1 year	55% of x	$82,000
Stratum I	1–3 months day	31% of x	$47,000

Note: In the above example 'x' = $150,000.
In practice, the organization will set 'x' based on market rates of pay and profiitiability.

So, in theory, once the rate of pay for a stratum III role is set, the pay for all other levels can be determined. This research has been confirmed by others on over twenty separate occasions.

In practice, using stratum levels for pay is difficult, but not impossible. Inhibitors to using this method include:

- The remuneration industry drives various methods of valuing work, and using reward as "motivation". Each claim to be the best.
- Unions often negotiate rates of pay in excess of value and market rates. While these tend to be at the lower stratum levels, they do impact the ratios of fairness at higher levels. For example, it is not uncommon to have pay compression between supervisor/team leader roles and manager roles.
- Unions negotiate pay levels up to middle management (especially for government sector organizations).
- The market rates of pay in a number of countries have driven senior executive pay to levels that are not justified (or fair).

- Skill shortages can distort "felt fair pay" when pay rates are pulled higher to attract or retain special skills.

The main point to remember is the concept of equity and "felt fair pay". While the exact dollar relativities are not that important, it is important to understand pay inequity will cause issues so each organization needs to be aware of the consequences. High CEO pay driven by out of control markets impact on the whole organization, not just the shareholders.

Each organization needs to determine the best method of implementing internal equity of pay to ensure pay is "felt fair". Jaques has provided the only independently tested method for determining "felt fair pay". Attempting to mirror this work will result in better internal equity of pay and a feeling of fairness.

ii. Differential pay.

The third question people ask is relates to being recognized and rewarded for performance effectiveness when compared to others – Am I rewarded for my effort? People expect to be rewarded for their effort and they expect to be rewarded differently to others. Linking compensation to individual performance effectiveness is important but needs care. Having strong direct links with the reward system does carry risk. For example:

- Does the organization have the right measures and targets?
- Does it have reliable data for the measures?
- Could unintended and unexpected consequences arise from the way the targets for the measures are achieved?
- Did the employee's manager support or hinder the employee's achievement of their objectives?

- What are the impacts of the working organization, i.e. its structure and systems of work and managerial leadership, on the employee's personal effectiveness?

Currently there is widespread and increasing use of bonuses as a tool for driving organizational performance improvement, especially at the executive level. However, there is no conclusive research proving that bonuses are effective at improving organizational performance. This approach to remuneration management often reflects, in part, the views of the CEO or board. But do they work?

While there appears to be universal acceptance of the importance of differential pay based on an individual's performance effectiveness, there are legitimate arguments around the usefulness of individual bonus systems. This debate centers on the basic beliefs about human motivation and work. Are people basically lazy and need to be urged to work? If an employee's pay is established properly as "felt fair pay" then why have a bonus system?

Proponents of bonus systems argue that bonuses:

- Are an effective way of getting people to focus on key objectives.
- Are a powerful tool for sending a message and aligning people with organizational objectives.
- Are an effective method of rewarding superior performance (even where they do not see it necessarily as a means of driving performance).
- Do not lock in salary costs and pay increases because the incentive must be re-earned.

Critics argue that:

- Employees in organizations can only be held accountable for doing their best in working toward their goals. As an employee's performance effectiveness is impacted by the performance effectiveness of their own manager and other organizational factors, such as structure and systems of work, they cannot be fully held to account for outcomes.

- In the absence of disciplined task assignment and other related managerial practices, no bonus pay system can be made fair. Better results can be gained with improved goal setting, as poor goal setting may result in goal under-achievement, despite the best efforts of the employee, or goal over-achievement with little effort.
- If employees are engaged to do their best, i.e. to work to their full potential, then it is illogical to attempt to reward for greater performance.
- External influences, such as market conditions and supplier issues, are outside the employees' control and can significantly impact outcomes.
- Bonuses can cause friction, a sense of injustice and can undermine team solidarity.
- Employees become too focused on the incentive at the cost of the long-term success of the organization.
- Required outcomes are not always clear, can change or are not as expected. What happens if the strategy was wrong or needs to be adjusted mid-term?
- Bonus schemes can be compromised more than a standard pay system because employees quickly come to see them as disconnected with reality. This causes cynicism and possible "gaming" of the bonus scheme (e.g. the employee bidding down targets against the manager bidding them up).
- There are additional administration costs for bonus systems.
- Often executives are being rewarded for short-term operational work rather than long-term strategic work. While each level of work is performed over different

timeframes, most bonus systems are annually based and don't hold executives to account for long-term sustained growth via multi-year performance targets.

There may be an argument that reasonable long-term incentives are suitable for some executive levels, but only if they relate to goals set according to level of work and time span of task, as outlined in the table below.

Level of work	Type of work	Time span	Level of employee
V	Business direction	5–10 years	CEO/Managing director
IV	Strategic delivery	2–5 years	General manger
III	Operational direction	1–2 years	Functional manager

Furthermore, many employees do not like individual bonus systems. The main reasons being:

- They may not be reflected in their superannuation, pension or retirement benefits.
- It is difficult to plan individual finances around a bonus.
- Financial institutions often do not consider bonuses in their criteria for loans.
- They can be withdrawn at any time.
- Outcomes can be influenced by factors outside their control.
- Goals may be just missed, but they lose all their bonus.
- The flow-down effect from their manager trying to achieve their goal, i.e. "I already work hard now. How much harder do you want?"

The establishment of any reward system requires an understanding of people in a work environment. The Leadership Framework believes that people are naturally motivated to work, work is something people value and people come to work to do their best. People do not need to be *motivated* per se.

If a team member's performance drops, then it is an issue for the manager (requiring assessment of the cause and an intervention). The cause may be outside of the control of the team member, such as organizational structure, systems of work, the capability of the employee's manager, unclear task assignment, etc. If this is accepted then it is difficult to punish a person and not give them a bonus because of this.

Note: Performance-based remuneration systems that link pay increases to the attainment of satisfactory performance effectiveness should not be confused with bonus systems for individual achievement of goals or targets. So, yes, reward higher performers with higher pay but do not use bonus systems as a motivator for strategy implementation.

b) Talent systems.

No strategy can be better than the people who are accountable to implement it. The aim is to ensure the organization has the right level of knowledge, skills and experience to implement the strategy.

Often, with a change in direction, new skills may be required so changes to attraction, recruitment or selection standards or processes may be needed. Where there is time, employee development could be an option.

Typical development areas include:

- Management development: This includes all aspects of leadership skills so that managers can build and lead an effective team. It includes skills for strategy implementation, role design, systems design and continuous improvement.
- Skills programs: Skills programs define the specific knowledge and skill requirements for identified tasks

(or for a role made up of several tasks) where there is a need to conform to legal, regulatory or organisationally specified standards of performance.

- Talent management: Talent management seeks to match individuals to appropriate roles and provides opportunities for the development of all employees to their maximum potential to meet current and future business needs.

Key Concepts

- Critical to successful strategy implementation is the role of the manager. Leadership is about creating a working environment that both enables and supports strategy implementation.
- To perform their role, managers must have a coherent and integrated framework for managerial leadership. Without such a framework, managers will not have a theoretical or practical basis for what they must do and how they do it. Providing a managerial leadership framework is a key accountability of the CEO.
- The design of the manager and team member roles, with the required working relationship, is essential for an organization to operate effectively.
- The role of a manager *is to achieve the business goals set for them and, at the same time, provide an environment that allows their staff to be effective and satisfied with their work while developing their full potential.* To do this, managers are specifically accountable for:
  - ➢ The output and behavior of their team.
  - ➢ Building and leading an effective team, so that each member is fully committed to and capable of moving in the established direction.
  - ➢ Continuous improvement of work processes and methods.

- Managers perform their accountabilities by effectively delivering the performance management sequence. This sequence starts with effective role design, followed by selection for the role, then induction of the individual into the role. It continues while the individual is working in the role.
- To do their work and fulfil their accountabilities, the design of the manager role must be provided two types of authorities:
  - Work authorities.
  - Role authorities (managerial).
- All team members are accountable to work effectively with their manager, team members and others in the organization. To do this, team members, at all levels, have five accountabilities to their manager. These accountabilities are:
  - Fulfil commitments made.
  - Bring their full capability to work.
  - Continue to develop their performance effectiveness.
  - Provide their manager with feedback.
  - Work together productively.
- Good People Management Systems are needed to support effective managerial leadership. The People Management System includes processes to develop the organizational structure, create roles, select and induct new employees, assign and assess work, reward and develop people and provide fair treatment.
- While the whole People Management System is important for effective managerial leadership, several key areas typically come into play for strategy implementation. These are the reward system and the talent systems, i.e. attraction and development.

Tips for Getting Started

1. Review the section on the role of the manager and team members. How has this been implemented in your organization? Can you make improvements for your team?
2. Read *Leading People – The 10 Things Successful Managers Know and Do* by Peter Mills. This book will provide you with a greater understanding of managerial leadership and the role of managers in working organizations.

Additional information available at www.theleadershipframework.com.au

1. Matching accountability with authority.
2. Creating effective roles and putting good people in them.
3. Role, accountability and authority of managers-once-removed.
4. Role, accountability and authority of project managers.
5. Role, accountability and authority of supervisors/team leaders.
6. Role, accountability and authority of peer leaders.
7. Ensuring the consistency and quality of leadership.
8. Ensuring fair treatment and justice.
9. Recognize and reward good work.
10. Develop team capability.

Chapter 10

Summary

STRATEGY IMPLEMENTATION is about converting strategic objectives into initiatives and effectively implementing them. This requires effective leadership at all levels in the organization. Effective leadership is not just about setting direction, it is also about creating a working environment that both enables and supports strategy implementation.

To successfully implement a strategy, leaders must:

a) Define the strategy.

The aim is to clearly articulate where the organization currently is, where it is planning to be and what it is going to do to get there. Using the outputs of the strategic planning process, the senior leadership team clarifies the organization's strategic objectives by:

- Describing the strategy in a way that employees can understand and support it.
- Providing clear measures and targets so that expected levels of future performance are understood.
- Creating fully funded and resourced initiatives to move the organization toward the required objective.

Clearly defining the strategy assists employees connect to it and sets the context for each person's work.

b) Align the organization.

The aim of organizational alignment is to enable and support success. This is achieved by:

i.   Allocating accountability and authority.

The CEO allocates accountability, with the necessary authority to deliver each strategic initiative, to members of the senior leadership team. Where an initiative requires action from multiple divisions, the CEO breaks the initiative into components and allocates individual tasks to each VP/general manager.

ii.   Connecting planning to budgeting.

Resources to complete each initiative are assigned and then allocated to a member of the senior leadership team through the budgeting process. Alternatively, a separate strategy execution budget may be created. This decision comes down to how the organization wants to monitor strategy implementation.

iii. Aligning the working organization.

Critically, the whole working organization must be aligned to both enable and support strategy implementation. This requires the senior leadership team to ensure the organization's structure, systems of work and managerial leadership framework are designed to support strategy implementation.

▪ Structure

An organization's structure provides the shared understanding of the working relationships that exist among people whose work must be aligned and integrated to deliver the organization's products and services. Therefore, the organization's structure and roles must be designed to support strategy implementation. Clear roles with defined working relationships and appropriate accountability and authority for work are needed to provide the basic rules of engagement for people to work together, i.e. who needs to work with whom, who makes the decision and who carries it out.

In designing the horizontal structure, the issue is: what work needs to be put together and what should be separated? The grouping and separation of work will vary from organization to organization, with each needing to make its own decisions based on its strategy, size, complexity and business requirements. As points of failure often occur at the handoff points between functions, the CEO must define where the accountability and authority for one area finishes and the where it commences for the next.

In relation to the vertical structure, a layer of management must only be created where work is more complex than the work of the role below. This is so each level of management can add value to the roles immediately below and that the right work is performed at the right level by the right people.

Note: Principles and practices for organizational design are available on The Leadership Framework member's website.

- Systems of Work

The effective design and deployment of systems of work is essential for strategy implementation. Systems of work:

> Facilitate work across functions, across teams and within teams.
> Provide the standardizing methods and boundaries for work to be done.
> Align people and work with legislation, social norms and the organization's values.
> Allow the leadership team to monitor and verify that the organization's purpose and strategy are being achieved in accordance with its cultural, ethical and moral standards.
> Critically influence the ability of people to do their best work.

Prioritizing the design, review and deployment of a system of work should be based on the organization's strategic requirements, i.e. what systems of work are key for strategy delivery. There are, however, four systems that organizations must get right for successful strategy implementation. These are the System of Systems, the Strategy Implementation System, the Organizational Design System and the People Management Systems.

It is important to note that, while the whole People Management System is important for effective managerial leadership, two areas typically come into play for strategy implementation. These are the reward system and the talent systems, i.e. attraction and development.

Note: Principles and practices for the design and implementation of systems of work are available on The Leadership Framework member's website.

- Managerial Leadership

Effective strategy implementation requires effective managerial leadership and effective managerial leadership requires a holistic framework that integrates all aspects of the working organization, i.e. structure, roles and role relationships and systems of work with managerial leadership. If managerial leadership is not integrated with structure and systems of work, even good managers will find it difficult to overcome a misaligned work environment.

In The Leadership Framework, the role of a manager is to *achieve the business goals set for them and, at the same time, provide an environment that allows their staff to be effective and satisfied with their work while developing their full potential.* To do this, managers are specifically accountable for:

> ➤ The output and behavior of their team.
> ➤ Building and leading an effective team, so that each member is fully committed to and capable of moving in the established direction.

> ➤ Continuous improvement of work processes and methods.

To perform these accountabilities, managers must build strong, two-way manager-team member working relationships. They do this by effectively delivering the performance management sequence. This sequence starts with effective role design, followed by selection for the role, then induction of the individual into the role. It continues while the individual is working in the role.

Note: Principles and practices for effective managerial leadership are available on The Leadership Framework member's website.

c) Cascade and deploy the strategy.

The aim of cascading the strategy is to move work from a high level in the organization to those who do the work. This begins by communicating the big picture to all employees so they have context for their work. Then managers of managers integrate the work of their team of teams. They hold meetings with their individual immediate subordinate managers and their team members to communicate how the functions are to work together to deliver the required outcomes. They ensure their team of managers collaborate constructively to achieve the plan of the business unit.

Every manager at every level then reviews the initiatives they have been allocated and they discuss implementation with their team. They discuss *what* must be achieved, *why* it must be achieved and *how* it is to be achieved. The manager then allocates this work to team members.

When assigning tasks, managers ensure each task has the context, purpose, quality and quantity required of the task. There must also be a clear understanding of the time the task is due and the resources are available for task completion.

d) Monitor and assure strategy implementation.

Monitoring and assuring the strategy is the final step in strategy implementation. The leadership team develops data collection, analysis and reporting systems to enable the effective monitoring of objectives and initiatives.

Regular strategy review meetings are held to discuss implementation of initiatives. At these meetings, attendees assess the progress of strategy delivery and assess the causes of implementation problems. Corrective actions are recommended and accountability assigned.

In addition to strategy review meetings, the senior leadership team holds strategy assessment meetings to test, validate and modify the hypotheses embedded in the strategy based on the latest information.

Monitoring strategy implementation is also part of the ongoing performance planning process for all employees. Goals and tasks are assessed as part of every employee's ongoing performance effectiveness review, identifying any problems or impediments to achieving tasks.

In addition to this, managers ensure team members are engaged in strategy implementation by continually addressing the four key questions that all employees can be expected to have:

- Where are we going?
- What's my role?
- How will my performance be judged?
- Where am I going?

Finally

Good strategy implementation is the result of the thousands of decisions made every day by employees acting in accordance with the information they have. Successful strategy implementation can only be achieved where employees understand what needs to be done, have clear accountability and authority for action, have the necessary resources to perform their work and where the working organization is designed to support their actions. Without clear direction and an effective strategy implementation process, that integrates all aspects of the working organization, an organization's strategy may not be delivered and the causes of failure will not be clear.

Learn More

Learn more about implementing business strategy or The Leadership Framework by joining The Leadership Framework Network at **www.theleadershipframework.com.au**, either as an individual or organization, and gain access to:

1. Information, tools, templates, and checklists that will support you to implement business strategy.
2. Additional information on how to:
    - Improve managerial leadership, at all levels.
    - Create effective organization structures.
    - Create constructive working environments.
    - Improve workforce capability.
    - Identify and develop talent.
    - Improve safety performance.
    - Create effective teams.
    - Build teamwork.
    - Build mutual trust and strong manager-employee working relationships.
    - Improve employee engagement.
    - Manage change.
    - Improve work systems and processes.
    - Manage performance issues.

Alternatively:

1. Read *Leading People — The 10 Things Successful Managers Know and Do* by Peter Mills to gain a better

understanding of the role, accountabilities and authorities of managers and learn how to build and lead an effective team.

2. Read *Don't Fix Me, Fix the Workplace – A Guide to Building Constructive Working Relationships* by Peter Mills to identify the main causes of workplace conflict and learn how to create the right working environment, which enables constructive working relationships and leads to productive work.

3. Arrange seminars/workshops at your workplace on any aspect of The Leadership Framework.

Appendix 1

The Leadership Framework

THE LEADERSHIP FRAMEWORK provides managers and organizations with a complete, holistic and coherent system of managerial leadership. It considers the organization as a purpose-built structure, with systems of work and specifically designed working relationships that enable people to work toward a common business purpose. The organization itself is activated or deployed by applying effective managerial leadership.

The Leadership Framework describes what all managers must know and must do. It clearly defines the requirements for leadership and sets practical and consistent standards expected of people leaders. Being a holistic framework it can be used to:

- Improve managerial leadership at all levels.
- Implement business strategy.
- Create effective organization structures.
- Improve workforce capability.
- Talent identification and development.
- Improve safety performance.
- Build effective teams and teamwork.
- Build mutual trust and strong manager-employee relationships.

- Improve employee engagement.
- Manage change.
- Improve work systems and processes.
- Manage performance issues.

The framework's three interconnecting parts provide a set of integrated principles and practices for the organization and for the individual.

Leading yourself is about understanding the role of the manager and how to work with others across the organization, building quality working relationships. It also comprises the essential requirements of what managers need to know about how to deal productively with workplace conflict and people differences.

Leading people is about the things managers must do on a day-to-day basis to manage their team. It comprises the minimum and essential requirements of all people managers from frontline managers up to, and including, the CEO/ managing director. It includes creating effective roles and filling them with good people, assigning and assessing work, rewarding and recognizing good work, building a capable team, continuous improvement and managing change and providing a safe place to work.

Leading the organization is about the additional requirements of managers occupying roles immediately above the frontline manager level. It involves designing and implementing fit for purpose workplace conditions, such as organizational structures and systems of work, to enable and support effective managerial leadership and productive work. Business strategy and building workforce capability is part of this.

At the framework's core are strong, two-way, trusting, working relationships, focused on achieving business goals.

Using The Leadership Framework enables organizations to operate effectively to deliver strategy. It enables managers to build high-performing teams focused on achieving business objectives. It also enables managers to develop team members to their full potential and be personally successful.

Origin of The Leadership Framework

At the framework's foundation is a body of knowledge known as Requisite Organization; requisite meaning what is required by the natural order of things. The concepts and principles were originally developed by Dr. Elliott Jaques and Lord Wilfred Brown and are based on significant research and practice around the world. This research considers organizational design as a purpose-built structure, with systems of work and defined working relationships that enable people to work toward a common business purpose. The organization itself is activated by applying effective managerial leadership practices.

The original Leadership Framework was developed by Barry and Sheila Deane from PeopleFit Australasia, who simplified and condensed Jaques' principles and practices.

Using PeopleFit's work, I have complemented, modified and updated it using the research of others and from my own extensive experience:

- In senior Human Resources roles across a range of industries, both in the private and public sector.
- Working directly with my own team as a leader on setting goals and improving performance.
- As an advisor and coach to CEOs, managers and non-manager roles in organizations.

The Leadership Framework is the only complete framework for people management.